SUSTAINABLE ESOPS

Plan design, governance, culture, and finance

SUSTAINABLE ESOPS

Plan design, governance, culture, and finance

Corey Rosen

The National Center for Employee Ownership · Oakland, California

This publication is designed to provide accurate and authoritative information regarding the subject matter covered. It is sold with the understanding that the publisher is not engaged in rendering legal, accounting, or other professional services. If legal advice or other expert assistance is required, the services of a competent professional should be sought.

Legal, accounting, and other rules affecting business often change. Before making decisions based on the information you find here or in any publication from any publisher, you should ascertain what changes might have occurred and what changes might be forthcoming. The NCEO's Web site (including the members-only area) and newsletter for members provide regular updates on these changes. If you have any questions or concerns about a particular issue, check with your professional advisor or, if you are an NCEO member, call or email us.

Sustainable ESOPs: Plan Design, Governance, Culture, and Finance
Corey Rosen

Book design by Scott Rodrick

Copyright © 2015 by The National Center for Employee Ownership. All rights reserved. No part of this book may be reproduced or transmitted in any form or by any means, electronic or mechanical, including photocopying, recording, or by any information storage and retrieval system, without prior written permission from the publisher.

The National Center for Employee Ownership
1629 Telegraph Ave. Suite 200
Oakland, CA 94612
Phone (510) 208-1300
Fax (510) 272-9510
www.nceo.org

Printed August 2015

ISBN: 978-1-938220-35-7

Contents

1. Introduction   1
2. Sustainable Distribution Policies   9
3. Sustainable Repurchase Policies   21
4. Valuation Issues   37
5. Leadership Succession and ESOP Sustainability   45
6. Solutions for the Have/Have-Not Problem   63
7. Sustainable ESOP Governance   71
8. Communicating ESOPs   93
9. Creating and Growing an Ownership Culture   113
10. Strategy and ESOP Sustainability   139
    Ken Ritterspach

    Appendix: Additional Resources   157

    About the Author   159

    About the NCEO   160

Chapter 1

Introduction

The Antioch Company in Yellow Springs, Ohio, was one of the first US companies to set up a profit sharing plan. The company's leaders had a strong commitment to employees, one passed down through three generations of ownership. It made sense, then, that in 1979, Lee Morgan decided to set up an ESOP to transfer minority ownership in Antioch to the roughly 160 employees of the printer of book plates and other specialty printing.

In 1985, Antioch bought a failing scrapbook company in Minnesota that eventually became Creative Memories. That company, which sold largely through home parties, took off, and by 2003, the stock value that had been $4 in 1975 became $640 and employment went up 1,000%.

That same year, the ESOP borrowed money to buy all the remaining shares, and Antioch became a 100% ESOP-owned S corporation. As part of that transaction, employees who terminated employment after October 1, 2004, were guaranteed a share price of at least $841. In addition, Antioch's distribution policy called for employees to be paid out one year after termination.

The scrapbook business was cyclical, however, and started a sharp downturn soon after. With hundreds of employees having six-figure accounts or more in the ESOP, many decided to leave to preserve as much value as they could. The huge cash flow required to cash out ex-employees, and the falling revenues at Creative Memories, forced Antioch into bankruptcy. Litigation soon followed, with a settlement ultimately reached.

Antioch's appraisal firm never factored the emerging repurchase obligation and floor price protection into value, even though the repurchase obligation required substantially higher contributions to the ESOP than would have been the case for a more typical retirement plan. Moreover, the floor price plan was poorly structured, guaranteeing a fixed minimum amount rather than the more recommended approach of guaranteeing the price at the time of the new acquisition debt minus any decline in value unrelated to the debt, such as the steep decline in revenues from Creative Memories.

Had Antioch followed a more conservative distribution policy, factored the repurchase into value, and used a more appropriate floor-price guarantee, it might still be an ESOP today. The bankruptcy was particularly tragic given the Morgan family's commitment to the values of employee ownership.

Antioch is a particularly stark example of an ESOP that proved unsustainable. Distribution and repurchase policies are key elements in making an ESOP sustainable, but sustainability also requires attention to communications, culture, avoiding the have/have-not problem, corporate strategy, leadership transition, and corporate governance.

Why Sustainability Has Become a Major Concern for ESOP Companies

Sustainability, largely ignored until the 1990s, has become one of the most talked-about ESOP issues. Some ESOPs were meant as one-time transactions to buy out an owner, often a minority owner. After the debt was repaid, the ESOP would be terminated and remaining owners would assume 100% control. Other ESOP companies saw the plan as a waystation to an eventual acquisition. Most ESOP companies in the 1990s had a minority of their stock owned by the plan, and only 4% were 100% ESOP-owned. While there were many companies that were committed to ownership for the long term, most plans were relatively young and had not yet faced the emerging issues of handling repurchase obligations in the long term, dealing with the have/have-not problem, or finding new leaders who would fit the ownership culture. Indeed, the whole idea of an ownership culture was itself new. In the 1970s and 1980s, the prevailing view was that communicating the ESOP well would be enough to motivate employees to create improved corporate performance.

All this started to change in the 1990s. Experience and research done by the NCEO and others in the mid- and late-1980s showed that communication was not enough. Companies needed to create high-involvement structures so that employees could regularly share ideas and information—and the ESOP companies that did that performed far better as a result. Culture change is a slow process, however, so companies needed to make a long-term commitment.

Even more important was the passage of laws allowing ESOPs in S corporations, where the profits attributable to the ESOP are exempt from federal (and usually state) income taxes. This created a sea change in the ESOP community. ESOPs owning 100% of the company became common, accounting for perhaps a third of all plans by 2014, a number that is still growing.

Because of the unique tax benefits S corporation ESOPs provide, there is much more incentive than there has been in the past to remain an ESOP in the long term. Moreover, as companies moved to 100% ESOP ownership, they became even more concerned with creating and sustaining an effective ownership culture than they had been when ESOP ownership percentages were smaller.

As a consequence, ESOP sustainability is a perennially popular topic at ESOP conferences. Much of the discussion focuses on internal dynamics in the ESOP, particularly:

- How to manage the repurchase obligation to make sure companies can buy back shares over time without causing excessive financial stress.
- Creating distribution policies that can balance cash flow preservation with opportunities to repurchase shares at opportune times.
- Creating rebalancing and account segregation policies to make sure that mature ESOPs can have shares to allocate to newer employees.

All of these considerations are critically important, but they are only part of the story. A truly sustainable ESOP company also has a strategy to maintain an effective employee ownership culture and a profitable business model. In particular, this means:

- Developing an effective risk management program.
- Creating a governance system consistent with being a long-term ESOP company.
- Having a leadership succession strategy to develop and promote new leaders not just at the executive level, but for all critical jobs.

- Growing an employee ownership culture of high employee involvement and open-book management.
- Implementing a corporate strategy that allows for sustainable growth, whether internally and/or through acquisitions.

This book looks at each of these issues. Of course, each of them merits much longer discussion on their own, so this book provides references to other material that explores each topic in depth. The key issues discussed in the following chapters are briefly summarized below.

Key Issues

Distribution Polices

ESOP distribution policies are often boilerplate insertions into plan documents that allow a company to put off distributions until the latest the law allows. The logic behind this approach is that delaying the repurchase obligation maximizes cash flow, allowing the company to grow rather than devote resources to repurchase. For companies that think they will eventually be sold, delaying can be a particularly good strategy because as the obligation grows in later years, someone else will take care of it when a sale occurs.

But for companies that want to stay ESOP-owned over the very long term, delaying repurchases may not be a good idea. If stock value is rising faster than a company's cost of money, delay only makes the eventual costs higher. Many ESOP companies pay out sooner than required, based on that theory and/or a desire to make the ESOP seem more relevant to people by showing them that they will not have to wait as long to get their money. A sustainable distribution policy, therefore, is one that is crafted to the company's specific situation. Within limits, distribution policies can also be written to allow some degree of flexibility and discretion.

Another key decision is who should repurchase the shares. Shares can be bought by the company and retired and/or recontributed to the ESOP, or the company can have the ESOP buy back the shares, often with cash contributions made for this purpose to the trust. Companies need to perform regular repurchase analyses and consult with their advisors to come up with a plan that works best.

The Have/Have-Not Problem: Share Strategies, Releveraging, Rebalancing, and Account Segregation

As ESOPs mature, they can develop a "have/have-not" problem that makes sustaining an ownership culture very difficult. Employees in the early years may have benefitted from large annual contributions used to acquire company stock. Once all the shares are acquired, new employees only get shares from forfeitures or recycled repurchased shares. That may not be enough to give them a real sense of ownership. Many ESOP companies now address the have/have-not problem with account segregation and/or rebalancing accounts. Account segregation provides that when employees terminate, their account balances are transferred to cash until their distribution begins. Their shares are then reallocated to all participants. With rebalancing, at the end of each plan year, the company uses cash in the accounts of employees with cash to buy shares from those with shares in such a way that at the end of the procedure, everyone has the same percentage of stock and cash. In 2010, the IRS made it clear that segregation is allowable, provided certain rules are met. The plan document must allow for segregation for it to be done.

Other approaches to consider are allocating forfeitures so as to favor newer employees, contributing more shares to the trust, making additional share acquisitions, and releveraging the ESOP.

Valuation

One of the most important issues affecting sustainability is making sure the repurchase obligation is reflected in the appraisal. Appraisers have argued that the company could always just be sold and, in any event, the law required the appraisal to be based on what a willing buyer would pay. Since that buyer would extinguish the repurchase obligation, the argument went, it could not be factored into the valuation. In recent years, however, the consensus has strongly shifted so that almost all institutional fiduciaries and most lawyers and appraisers believe that the repurchase obligation should be a factor. The argument now is that if an ESOP is a long-term benefit, fiduciaries should look at what would keep the plan viable over many years so that future employees will benefit as well. By not factoring in repurchase obligations, the argument goes, people who leave earlier get overpaid and those leaving later get underpaid. By factoring in the repurchase obligation, ESOP companies can avoid overpaying for shares and creating a cash crunch that may require a sale or, worse, bankruptcy.

Ownership Culture and Communications

In the mid-1980s, the NCEO did an extensive research project on what makes some ESOP companies perform better than others. The answer was clear: the best-performing companies had extensive employee involvement systems—open-book management, employee teams, ad-hoc employee problem-solving groups, and other structured ways to get employees to contribute ideas. Open-door policies were not enough. Effective communications about the ESOP mattered, but were not sufficient. The least participative ESOPs, which had raised employee expectations about their role in the company but not met them, showed a decline in performance; meanwhile, the most participative ESOP companies improved their post-ESOP performance by 6% to 11% per year over what would have been expected. Creating a sustainable ESOP requires that companies create these kinds of cultures.

To sustain an ownership culture, companies need to:

1. Provide ownership education that teaches people how the company makes money and their role in making that happen.
2. Share performance data about how the company is doing overall and how each work group contributes to that.
3. Train people in business literacy so they understand the numbers the company shares.
4. Share profits through bonuses, profit sharing, or other tools.
5. Build employee involvement not just by allowing employees to contribute ideas and information but making that part of their everyday work organization through teams, feedback opportunities, devolution of authority, and other structures.

Communications are also an essential element of an ownership culture. People need to know what an ESOP is (and isn't). The best communications programs have a few key characteristics:

1. They provide frequent small bites of information. A company might have a piece on ESOPs in each newsletter, or a monthly e-mail, or a one-page explanation of some aspect of ESOPs that it sends to people every month. These small chunks of information are easier to digest. The regular repetition, however, is itself a powerful communication tool reminding people about being a part of an ESOP company.
2. They have an ESOP communications committee or team that includes nonmanagement employees who develop approaches that are well-suited to the particular population.
3. They have an orientation to the ESOP program for new employees and invite existing ones who want a refresher to sit in.
4. They use multiple modes of communication. Some people learn visually, others by reading, others by having discussions.
5. They make communications as interactive as possible. For instance, a company might have a program on its internal website that lets people plug in some realistic numbers to see how their accounts might grow over time. Others have some kind of ESOP game at annual meetings, such as ESOP Jeopardy, to get people thinking about the ESOP.
6. They celebrate and have fun.

Leadership Succession

No company is sustainable unless it has a leadership succession and development policy that works. We tend to think of leadership succession in terms of CEOs and a few other corporate officers, but leadership succession also matters throughout the company among any employees who can assume leadership roles—supervisors, team leaders, and key technical people, for instance.

It is always important, of course, that new leaders have the specific skills needed for their jobs. But most leaders in an ESOP company need cultural skills as well. They need genuinely to buy into the company's ownership culture. If the company is the kind of open-book, high-engagement culture described above, leaders need to see the nurturing of that culture as one of the most essential elements of their jobs. Many

CEOs we at the NCEO have talked to say cultural skills are the most essential element.

Governance

As ESOP companies start to think more about being employee-owned as a long-term objective, they have also started to focus more on what kinds of governance structures will work best for them. In the past, ESOP companies were governed not much differently from any private company, with boards made up of insiders and/or family members and corporate officers serving as plan fiduciaries. While this is still true for many ESOP companies, a growing number are adding outside board members and independent trustees. There are good arguments to be made over whether independent plan fiduciaries are critical to sustainability, but there is a broad consensus among ESOP advisors that having outside board members is a good idea.

Strategy and Risk Management

ESOP companies are no different from any company in needing to develop appropriate short- and long-term strategies and approaches to risk management. They need to add to the mix, however, how the repurchase obligation will affect strategy, how potential acquisitions will fit into the corporate culture, how layoffs will be handled, and other considerations unique to ESOP companies.

Conclusion

As more and more ESOP companies plan to stay employee-owned (or have been) for decades, sustaining ownership in a way that is financially manageable and culturally effective requires a great deal of time and work. The popularity of this topic at meetings is indicative of just how much there is to know. But given the extraordinary tax benefits of an S corporation ESOP, plus the demonstrated impact of a strong ownership culture, it is clear that sustaining an ESOP long-term is well worth the effort.

Chapter 2

Sustainable Distribution Policies

Antioch Publishing had long been a leader in sharing the rewards of business ownership, setting up a formal deferred profit sharing plan soon after its founding in 1926. It was one of the first companies to adopt an ESOP after the Employee Retirement Income Security Act of 1974 (ERISA) was passed. For many years, it continued on a steady, successful course as a mid-sized printer of calendars and book plates. Then in 1987 it acquired Creative Memories, a scrapbook producer that sold its products through home parties. Creative Memories was in bankruptcy at the time but took off after the acquisition, and Antioch grew 1,000% over the next several years. The scrapbook business was cyclical, however, and started a rapid downturn around 2006.

Antioch had a very liberal distribution policy that allowed employees to cash in a year after they left. Compounding the problem was that Antioch's appraiser did not factor the emerging repurchase obligation into the value of the shares (which this book's chapter on the repurchase obligation discusses in detail). Many employees had six- or even seven-figure accounts. Seeing the writing on the wall, hundreds decided to cash in while they could. Faced with a severe cash crunch trying to meet the repurchase obligation, Antioch was forced into bankruptcy.

In retrospect, a more conservative distribution policy would have discouraged people from jumping ship in the same numbers, and a more appropriate valuation technique would have lowered the stock price to reflect the emerging liability. But hindsight was too late for Antioch. The story was particularly tragic because the company had been so committed to not just staying employee-owned in the long term but being an exemplar of ownership culture.

Fortunately, few ESOP companies face these kinds of existential problems. But every ESOP company needs to think carefully about how its distribution policies are structured in order to be sustainable over not just the next several years, but for decades.

There are several key issues to consider in creating a sustainable distribution policy:

- Should the policy be hard-wired into the plan, or should the plan provide for the minimum requirements of the law but stipulate that a written and separate distribution policy could provide for a more liberal policy?
- When should distributions begin?
- Should distributions be in the form of stock or cash?
- Should distributions be in a lump sum or installments?
- Should you have an in-service distribution option?
- If you have an outstanding ESOP loan, how long is it prudent to delay repurchases?

This chapter covers each of these issues. The NCEO has a more detailed issue brief on distribution policies[1] for those looking for more information. At the end of this chapter, I look at the separate but related issues of how to make sure new employees get shares in mature ESOPs.

Should You Have a Separate Distribution Policy?

ESOP distribution policies are often boilerplate insertions into plan documents that allow a company the maximum flexibility in making distributions. They generally provide for the longest allowable delays in repurchase, although some plans are more liberal. The form of the distribution (stock or cash) and method (lump sum or installments) is also specified. Vesting rules typically provide for graded vesting over six years.

Many companies, however, write their plans to say that the plan will start distributions no later than a specified maximum time period, but a separate written distribution policy will govern the actual timing and

---

1. Corey Rosen, Rebecca Hoffman, and Cindy Prodoehl, *ESOP Distribution Policies* (NCEO, 2010) (see nceo.org/r/distribution).

form of distribution. The arguments for a separate distribution policy are that (1) the company does not have to amend its plan every time it wants to make a change, (2) the policy can build in some discretion for earlier payouts or a different form or method of payout, and (3) the discretion allowed the committee can make it easier to adapt to changes in economics and demographics. For instance, if a company has the cash, and its stock value is growing faster than its cost of money, buying more shares earlier makes the plan more financially sustainable. That same argument could apply to making distributions in cash rather than stock, especially in an installment distribution. If problems come up, the committee could go back to allowable delays.

An ESOP committee or other body is designated as responsible for the policy. If this committee decides that one of the purposes is to allow some discretion in the timing of distributions, there are a number of approaches it could take, as described below. To protect cash flow, however, the plan would be given discretion by the committee to delay payouts on a nondiscriminatory basis if the cash requirements of early payouts would put the company at financial risk. Nondiscriminatory here means there is no intent or pattern to favor more highly compensated employees.

Some variations on discretionary distributions might include:

- Paying people with balances under a certain amount sooner than those with more than that amount.

- Paying out all distributions within one year of termination (or two, three, or four) provided the company has a cash reserve of some amount in excess of the required amount in the ESOP and/or its balance sheet. Be cautious about this approach, however, as many experts believe that changing to a slower distribution from a faster one can be an ERISA violation.

- Paying out sooner provided the ESOP committee (or sometimes the board) determines that doing so does not impose a financial risk on the company.

- Paying out sooner up to a certain maximum total per participant, provided the ESOP committee (or sometimes the board) determines that doing so does not impose a financial risk on the company.

- Starting payouts after one year on an annual basis to a maximum of x dollars per year per person, such as $20,000, with a balloon payment after five years for the remaining amount.

The ESOP distribution policy could also provide that the company can change the form of distribution from stock to cash or vice versa, or in a lump sum instead of installments. The rules for vesting could also be changed (but see below). Changes in plan rules may also be an issue the board of directors needs to decide on (boards have the power to set plan rules, but can delegate them to the committee).

Legal opinion is divided on having a separate distribution policy. There are some changes that clearly can or cannot be made because of anti-cutback rules:

- Companies cannot lengthen the vesting schedule for people already in the plan (but they can for new participants).
- An ESOP sponsor can change from a lump-sum distribution to an installment distribution or vice versa.
- Companies can change the form of the distribution from stock to cash if the company's bylaws require that all or substantially all the stock be owned by employees or the company is an S corporation.

Whether companies can also lengthen the timing of distributions, such as from one year after separation to five years, is less clear, and experts do not agree on this issue. Some companies have done it, but some lawyers worry that the IRS has not specifically sanctioned this as an allowable exception to the anti-cutback rules. It may be more practical to limit any extension of the timing of distributions to non-vested participants. Changes must be made with advice of counsel.

Some advisors also say that discretion is per se a problem. Some would argue that if a company follows the same rules every year, it has created a de facto policy that employees should be able to rely on. A larger number, however, say that it is permissible to have a carefully crafted discretionary approach based on paying out sooner than required if there is sufficient cash to do so and the policy is in the best long-term interests of plan participants as long as it is done in a way that scrupulously avoids favoring more highly compensated participants, makes changes in policy the exception not the norm, and is done for well-documented and carefully discussed reasons.

When Should Distributions Begin?

Whether there is discretion in your rules or not, a decision needs to be made about when to start distributions. The most common distribution policy follows the maximum delays that the law allows. That means that when employees retire, die, or are disabled, the company must distribute their vested shares to them or their heirs not later than the last day of the plan year following the year of their departure. For employees leaving before reaching retirement age (where death or disability are not the reasons), distribution begins not later than the last day of the sixth plan year following the plan year of separation from service. C corporations can delay distributions (other than when general qualified plan distribution rules mandate an earlier date, as in the case of reaching retirement age) until after the ESOP loan is repaid, even if the loan is for a very long time (such as 15 to 20 years). (The applicability of the loan repayment delay to S corporations is discussed below.) Payments can be in substantially equal installments out of the trust over a period of no more than five years, or in a lump sum. In the installment method, a company normally pays out a portion of the stock from the trust each year. The value of that stock (and consequently the amount paid to the employee when the company buys back the stock) may go up or down over that time, of course. In a lump-sum distribution, the company buys the shares at their current value at the time of distribution, but it can pay for that purchase in installments over five years, as long as it provides adequate security and reasonable interest.

The logic behind this installment approach is that delaying the repurchase obligation as long as legally possible maximizes cash flow, allowing the company to grow rather than devote resources to repurchasing. For companies that think they will eventually be sold, delay can be a particularly good strategy because as the obligation grows in later years, someone else will take care of it when a sale occurs.

These policies may not make sense for many companies, however. If a company's stock value is rising faster than its cost of money, delay only makes the eventual repurchase costs higher. If a company has the available cash in the company or in the ESOP, paying out sooner can make the long-term repurchase obligation more manageable. The downside of a policy to pay out earlier is that it may be legally difficult to change to a slower distribution schedule if there is a cash crunch. It also could demotivate employees. Delaying payouts until many years after separation can make the ESOP seem less relevant to employees. Research on how people think about future benefits shows that they excessively discount for both the time value of money and the risk that the money might not be there.

Should Distributions Be in the Form of Stock or Cash?

ESOPs in S corporations, banks that are legally prohibited from redeeming or purchasing their own stock, and C corporations whose bylaws require that all or substantially all the stock be held by employees can make distributions in the form of cash, not shares. ESOPs in other companies can as well, but employees must have the option to require the distribution be in the form of stock.

Making distributions in the form of stock in an S corporation can put at risk S status if too many ex-employees become shareholders (S corporations can have no more than 100 shareholders) or transfer the shares to a nonqualified owner, most notably an IRA (unless the company or ESOP immediately repurchases the stock from the IRA and other conditions are met). A sustainable S corporation ESOP, therefore, will always make cash distributions as a rule.

For C corporations, share distributions get quickly translated into cash by participants, but if the distribution is in installments, distributing shares means the former employees see their stock value ride up and down with the company's fortunes. The argument for this on the company side is that not having to come up with the cash at the outset of the distribution, then paying it off in installments, delays and divides the need for cash into smaller chunks. On the other hand, if the stock price is going up faster than the cost of money, the company is making its situation more difficult. Many companies would also argue that former employees should neither benefit from company growth nor be at risk for declines in stock value.

Should Distributions Be in Installments or in a Lump Sum?

Installment payments can be made over a five-year period once distributions begin and can be in the form of stock or cash. (See above for the pros and cons of stock installments.) If the distribution is in cash, an installment payment must carry a reasonable rate of interest and must be secured by collateral, not just a promise.

Installment sales can manage cash effectively because the interest rate paid is almost certainly much lower than the company's internal rate of return on its capital. However, the collateral requirement may mean that the company's borrowing capacity is reduced somewhat. Employees would certainly also prefer a complete lump-sum payout.

While this decision is important, it has less impact on sustainability issues than other policies discussed here.

Should You Have an In-Service Distribution Before Required Diversification?

Some companies provide opportunities for employees to cash out or, more commonly, diversify into a 401(k) plan sooner than the required diversification rules. The reasons for this are similar to providing earlier than required distributions. If the company believes its stock price will go up faster than its cost of money, and it has good cash flow, early diversification can reduce long-term ESOP repurchase obligation costs. It also gives employees more control over their accounts, which may make them feel more like owners.

A typical arrangement might be to allow employees to diversify up to 25% of their account balance into their 401(k) plan every 10 years. If the 401(k) plan has a loan provision, this may also give employees access to needed cash, although financial advisors generally strongly advise against borrowing from a 401(k) plan except under the most demanding circumstances.

If You Have an Outstanding ESOP Loan, How Long Is It Prudent to Delay Repurchases?

C corporation ESOPs are allowed to delay starting distributions to terminating employees until the plan year after the plan year in which the loan is repaid, except where the general retirement plan rules mandate an earlier distribution. The interaction of this rule with installment distributions is complex. It is unclear whether the rule applies to S corporation ESOPs. Most attorneys believe that only a technical drafting error prevents this from clearly applying and recommend incorporating this provision in a plan document submitted for a letter of determination. If the IRS does not object, then they recommend proceeding with this provision. The delayed distribution rules apply only to the shares acquired by the loan, not to all shares in the plan.

Almost all leveraged ESOPs are structured with an external loan from the lender to the company and an internal loan from the company to the ESOP. The two loans can have different terms. Often, the external loan may be paid off over five to seven years, but the internal loan might extend to ten years or more. Companies may extend the internal loan to stay within the maximum allowable annual contribution rules. They may also do it to spread the benefit out more evenly over a longer period of time. Rather than allocating all the shares over five to seven years, a company might allocate more slowly to provide a sustainable level of employee benefits, typically about 5% to 15% of pay.

For employees who terminate before death or retirement age, the rules for delaying distributions until the loan is repaid are relatively straightforward. Distributions do not have to start until the plan year following the plan year in which the loan is repaid. Distribution must be completed in (1) the plan year following the plan year in which the loan is repaid or, if later, (2) the date distribution would have to be completed under the normal distribution rules specified in the plan document and/or distribution policy. If a participant leaves in 2019, for instance, and the loan is repaid in 2021, the participant could still have to wait until 2025 to get a distribution (assuming the plan year follows the calendar year), provided the plan and/or distribution policy provides that distributions do not have to start until five plan years after the end of the plan year the participant terminates or until after the loan is repaid, if later.

In the case of retirement age and death, the rules are more complicated because they interact with the general rules governing qualified plan distributions. Under those rules, distribution must start no later than the 60th day after the end of the plan year in which the later of these events occur: (1) the participant reaches age 65 or, if earlier, the plan's normal retirement age; (2) the year in which the employee retires; or (3) the 10th anniversary of participation in the plan. In the case of death, there are different rules depending on whether the death occurred before or after distributions have begun. (Note: These are general qualified plan rules that apply to all aspects of ESOP distributions, not just the deferral of distributions until after the loan is repaid.) These provisions can create somewhat complex interactions when employees leave before retirement age but after 10 years of service. Generally, in these cases, the normal ESOP rule would be trumped by the general rules and require a somewhat earlier distribution to begin.

There are a couple of important issues to consider when delaying the repurchase until after the loan is repaid. First, the Department of Labor may object to internal loans that are so long that they are aimed primarily at benefitting the company, not the employees.

Second, even if this is not an issue, delaying repurchase until after a very long loan is repaid causes multiple problems. First, it just builds repurchase obligation to larger and larger levels so that when distributions do begin, the company may find them overwhelming. Employees will also see the long lead time and discount the real benefit the ESOP can provide. Each of these makes the ESOP far less sustainable, both financially and culturally.

Getting Shares to New Employees

At some point, most ESOPs will have no further shares to buy from non-ESOP owners. Absent any other policies, that means new employees will typically only get shares from the recycling of shares that are acquired by the ESOP from former plan participants. In some cases, especially when the share value has been rising strongly, this will be enough to provide a significant ongoing stake. Often, however, it is not. For instance, a company may have been contributing 10% of pay to a leveraged ESOP for many years. When the debt is repaid, it may only need 3% of pay to buy back shares. Often, companies will make cash contributions to the plan to maintain a target compensation level. That means new employees have a small amount of stock relative to cash in their ESOP accounts. Companies can deal with this issue by just contributing new shares to the ESOP, although that will dilute other owners. Alternatively, companies can use rebalancing and/or account segregation. Chapter 6 discusses rebalancing and account segregation in detail, but because these issues affect distribution policies in that they can change the timing and level of distributions over time, they are briefly outlined here.

Rebalancing and account segregation are ways to use cash in the ESOP trust to buy shares from current employees (rebalancing) and former employees (account segregation). Shares are bought from some participants and replaced with cash allocated to other participants, who now get stock for their shares. Both, of course, require that ESOP trusts have cash in them. That could come from direct cash contributions and/or distributions paid into the plan.

In *rebalancing*, at the end of each year, shares are bought and sold in the trust so that everyone has the same percentage of stock and cash. In *account segregation,* when employees leave the company their shares are cashed out and reinvested in other assets, but distributions do not occur until some later date. While the company could just cash people out immediately or a short time after leaving, doing so may give employees an incentive to leave just to get their ESOP distributions. The shares that have been repurchased are reallocated to everyone in the plan. Both approaches raise fiduciary and practical issues that, while manageable, need to be addressed.

Either policy will affect distributions in both their form (employees will get more cash or all cash) and timing of when shares have to be paid for.

Conclusion

No one policy will be most sustainable for every company. Building in as much flexibility as possible within the law makes it easier to adjust policies as circumstances change. Companies need to perform regular repurchase analyses and consult with their advisors to determine what the financial implications of different policies will be. They also need to make sure employees understand the policies and why they are structured as they are. Adopting a standard boilerplate approach may seem appealingly easy and may indeed be the best policy for a company, but companies that want to sustain their ESOPs know that careful consideration and design is a wiser choice.

KEY TAKEAWAYS

- *Should the policy be hard-wired into the plan, or should the plan provide for the minimum requirements of the law but stipulate that a written and separate distribution policy could provide for a more liberal policy?* There is some disagreement about how much discretion is allowable, but most experts agree that a carefully crafted policy with reasonable and limited discretion is allowable and can help fit the distribution policy to a company's needs.

- *When should distributions begin?* Later may always seem more prudent, but earlier distributions can make sense if the stock value is rising quickly and the company has reliable cash flows or cash in the plan.

- *Should distributions be in the form of stock or cash?* Cash distributions are essential for S corporations, but C companies need to decide how much they want to put former participants at risk and/or allow them to participate in company growth.

- *Should distributions be in a lump sum or installments?* Lump-sum distributions can make sense for the same reason earlier than required distributions can.

- *Should you have an in-service distribution option?* For companies with strong stock price growth and available cash, this is an option worth considering.

- *If you have an outstanding ESOP loan, how long is it prudent to delay repurchases?* Delaying the start of repurchases to the end of a very long (over 10-year) ESOP loan creates a number of risks and can alienate employees.

Chapter 3

Sustainable Repurchase Policies

There is a famous experiment in which people are asked to watch a video and count the number of times a basketball is passed from one person to another. In the middle of the video, a person in a gorilla suit walks through the room, stops, pounds his chest, and walks out. Most people do not see the gorilla.

Early on in the development of ESOPs, the repurchase obligation was that gorilla. Most companies did little to plan for it. NCEO surveys showed that most companies did not do a repurchase obligation study and even fewer discussed repurchase obligation issues with their appraiser, much less factored it into the calculation of future free cash flow. Some well-known ESOP companies were forced to sell when their repurchase obligation became more than they could handle.

Fortunately, that has changed significantly. Most companies now have a repurchase analysis done periodically, and factoring the repurchase obligation into valuation, while not universal, is becoming the norm. According to NCEO research, only a very small number of ESOP terminations result from repurchase problems.

Crafting a sustainable repurchase policy is arguably the most important financial element of creating a sustainable ESOP. Part of this sustainability is based on distribution rules, covered in the previous chapter. This chapter looks at some of the key practical issues in how to fund the repurchase. It is not intended as a primer on what the rules for repurchase obligations are. Details on that can be found on our website and in much more detail in our book *The ESOP Company Repurchase Obligation Handbook*.[1] Rather, this chapter focuses on these key decisions:

- Getting the repurchase study right
- How does business strategy align with the repurchase obligation?

---

1. Judith Kornfeld et al., *The ESOP Repurchase Obligation Handbook* (NCEO, 2011) (see nceo.org/r/repurchase).

- Should the cash come from the company or contributions to the ESOP?
- Should you recycle or redeem shares?
- How should appraisals reflect the repurchase obligation?
- Should you refinance the ESOP?

Key Elements of a Sustainable Repurchase Obligation Assessment

Typically, it takes several years before a company begins to face any significant ESOP repurchase obligation. That may lull a company into complacency about predicting its future obligations and creating a program to manage them. It is far better to start the process early. We recommend that a company start to do repurchase obligation studies not later than four years after the start of its ESOP and do a reassessment at least every two years.

Companies can try to develop their own repurchase obligation projections, but unless there is staff specifically trained in this, we strongly recommend hiring a professional ESOP advisory firm. Often, this will be your plan administration firm, but there are also firms specializing in this field. The Service Provider Directory at the NCEO's website (www.nceo.org) provides a list of firms with ESOP repurchase study expertise. There is also commercially available software to do repurchase obligation analysis.

A repurchase study should focus on several key factors:

- Weights should be assigned to each participant based on age, vesting, and income. The participants can then be divided into three or more groups so that when an analysis is done, more emphasis is assigned to those individuals with the highest combination of age, vesting, and income.
- Vesting policies and the extent to which people are vested and will become vested over time should be calculated. Some companies, for instance, may have a significant percentage of employees who will never fully vest. The impact of that would be that the repurchase obligation is delayed (but not ultimately decreased) as their unvested shares get reallocated to other participants.

- Compensation and annual contribution levels will affect the repurchase obligation both in terms of helping to predict how much each participant will accumulate but also how this will change dynamically based on rates of increase in compensation and how contribution levels may change over time. Many ESOPs lower their contribution levels, for instance, after a loan is repaid, but if a company is making contributions to the ESOP to fund repurchases or recycling shares it buys back into the ESOP, the contribution level may remain relatively high.

- Stock value change projections should include what would happen in realistic scenarios. That should include the growth level that is most highly expected as well as at least one other scenario for both faster and slower growth (or even decline) that is realistically possible if not expected.

- Turnover rates for retirement and pre-retirement will affect the timing of repurchases. In larger companies, past patterns may be highly predictive; in smaller companies, someone in the company will often have a good sense of when people, at least those with higher account balances, might leave. All of this information can be entered into a repurchase spreadsheet.

- Distributions of earnings are often paid in S corporations directly into the trust. C corporations can do this as well, but do so much less often. This cash can be used to manage the repurchase obligation.

- Forfeiture policies will also affect the timing of repurchases. Some plans provide that forfeited shares are not immediately reallocated but held for five years to be available if the employee is reemployed.

- Plan provisions for how and when the distribution is paid will, of course, also have a significant impact.

Business Strategy and Repurchase Policy

Peter's Pie Company became a 100% ESOP 10 years ago. It has paid off its acquisition debt. It has good cash flow and a strong balance sheet. Alan Jones, Peter's CEO, knows there are opportunities for Peter's to expand, either by acquisition or opening a new facility in a nearby town.

But he's nervous. Under the more optimistic projections (at least from the participants' perspective) about the ESOP's repurchase obligation, the company will have enough cash to handle the obligation without dipping into its cash reserve. It would also have enough free cash flow left over to build up retained earnings more. Alan thinks they should pursue a conservative course and pass on growth, but his board is urging him to take advantage of the opportunities out there. They say that by doing that, Peter's can generate even more profit and use that to meet the repurchase needs and at the very least keep the balance sheet where it is. If things do get tight, the board argues, Peter's has a strong enough balance sheet to take on new debt to handle its cash obligations.

Smith's Ranch Products is 40% owned by its ESOP. The remaining owner would like to sell in the next few years. The current ESOP debt will be repaid in the next two years, and repurchase obligations will start to become meaningful in the next five years. Jill Cramer, Smith's CEO, is worried about meeting two (re)purchase needs—the ESOP's repurchase needs and the remaining owner's need to find a purchaser. One strategy would be to build more reserves, but, as at Peter's, there is also the chance that growing will create more profit. Another alternative is to attract an outside investor. That would keep Smith's from getting to 100% ESOP ownership and no taxes for many more years, but the new equity could make it easier to grow and handle current repurchase needs.

United Forging is in a different situation. Its business is stable, but there is little opportunity to grow. Profits are steady but unimpressive. The value of ESOP accounts is expected to grow, but slowly. Still, that cash flow demand means that United will have difficulty finding the new markets or retooling its operations that could make growth possible. United's board has suggested that a buyer be looked for, but its management team is committed to the ESOP and reluctant to act.

Morrison Professional Services just set up its ESOP. The repurchase obligation will not become significant for many years, although some relatively small costs could be incurred with the next few years. Morrison has a large acquisition debt to pay off, and chooses to focus on that for now, putting off issues of growth and building a reserve for repurchase.

None of these are actual companies, but the scenarios are very real. The presence of the repurchase obligation has an obvious and important impact on ESOP company strategy. In chapter 10, Ken Ritterspach looks in more detail at sustainable ESOP corporate strategy, but suffice it to say here that there is no obvious answer to what the best approach is. The dilemmas presented here are meant instead to highlight how important it is for ESOP companies to engage carefully in strategic decision-making that takes into account various repurchase scenarios.

Should the Cash Come from the Company or Contributions to the ESOP?

The legal obligation to repurchase shares rests with the company. The company can meet this obligation by using its own cash from reserves, cash flow, and/or borrowing money. Alternatively, the ESOP itself may repurchase the shares, although the company cannot make the ESOP do this.

The best strategy will depend in part on whether the company is a C or S corporation and what percentage of stock the plan owns. The key considerations for three different scenarios, a 100% ESOP-owned S corporation, a less-than-100% ESOP-owned S corporation, and a less-than-100% ESOP-owned C corporation (there are extremely few 100% ESOP-owned C corporations due to the overwhelming tax benefit to converting to S status) are outlined below.

In all these cases, the key concept is to let your sustainability policy drive how repurchases are handled and where the money comes from, rather than just following an approach that seems simpler or that you may have been told is "the way most people do it."

100% S Corporation ESOPs

S corporations that are 100% owned by the ESOP present a distinct set of issues:

- S corporations are pass-through entities, meaning that the owners of these companies pay taxes pro-rata to their ownership. The ESOP, however, is a nontaxable entity, so any profits attributed to the ESOP are not taxable. There are no income tax obligations, therefore, in 100% ESOP-owned S corporations.

- Because of the nontaxability of earnings in 100% ESOP-owned S corporations, there is no benefit from the deductibility of contributions to an ESOP to fund the repurchase obligation. As a result, it makes more sense for the company to repurchase the shares at the company level. For companies that want to keep their ESOP vibrant for the long term, this allows them to recontribute the shares based on a consistent and sustainable percentage of pay level. For instance, a company might target 10% of pay to be contributed to the ESOP annually. In some years, repurchased shares will be more than enough to meet this target, so the excess shares will be retained at the corporate level. In other years, there may be too few shares, so the company can use some of that reserve to make up the difference.

- 100% ESOP-owned S corporations that have reached that ownership level in a series of transactions typically would have distributions that have been made to the ESOP. That is because S corporation law requires that if a company makes distributions to any shareholder, it must make them pro-rata to all shareholders. Non-ESOP shareholders will want distributions to pay their taxes. The distributions made to the ESOP do not need to be used to pay taxes and thus accumulate over time. That can provide a substantial source of cash (that does not affect corporate cash flow) for handling repurchase obligations.

- Some S corporations use distributions to pay down the ESOP acquisition debt. The law requires these distributions to be allocated based on relative share balances for allocated shares, but they can be based on either relative share balances or the normal allocation formula for unallocated shares. It makes more sense to use the normal formula for unallocated shares because using the relative share balance approach means the "rich get richer" and newer employees get very little. It also hastens the repurchase obligation. Even using the normal formula for unallocated shares, however, will still mean that as the loan is paid down, more and more of the shares eventually get allocated to accounts of people who already have a lot of shares, and few shares will be allocated to newer employees. Because of this, a best practice is to use distributions to pay down debt only if necessary to avoid the annual contribution limits (and keep in mind that extending the internal loan term may allow for more sustainable annual contributions without the need for distributions).

Less-Than-100% S Corporation ESOPs

In a less-than-100% ESOP-owned S corporation, non-ESOP owners will have to pay income tax on their shares of company profits. Contributions to the ESOP, however, reduce taxable income reported to S corporation owners. Any cash that is contributed is allocated to employee accounts and must ultimately be distributed. So while the cash can be used in the interim to buy back shares, ultimately the company will have to replace it. Because the plan is buying back the shares, the shares are automatically reallocated to everyone else in the plan. That assures an ongoing source of share allocations for all participants, but if a company has a lumpy distribution pattern, with large amounts distributed one year and small amounts another, participants will be in something of a lottery for how much they get each year.

Alternatively, the company can redeem the shares and recontribute a consistent amount each year. Redemptions are not deductible expenses, but the (re)contributions are. If all the shares that are for sale have been paid for and no new shares are to be purchased, many companies will contribute additional cash to reach that level annually. For instance, repurchased and recontributed shares may equal 4% of pay in one year, but the company wants to contribute 10% per year to the ESOP, so another 6% is in cash. This cash can then be used to buy shares from an owner who wants to sell in the future and/or to meet future repurchase obligation needs.

Putting cash into the plan as it matures to fund some part of the repurchase obligation is often a good strategy in less-than-100% S corporation ESOPs. Not only does it provide a safety valve if the company has inadequate cash flow, but it also helps provide diversification for employees over time.

C Corporation ESOPs

The issues for any C corporation, no matter what percentage the ESOP owns, are much the same as for less-than-100% S corporation ESOPs.

Contributions of cash to the plan are deductible, but create a future obligation. Company repurchases are not deductible, but re-contributions of the shares to the plan are. The planning issues around how to choose would be the same as for less-than-100% S corporation ESOPs.

Some C corporation ESOPs also pay dividends on the shares, most often to go beyond the allowable annual contribution limits (dividends do not count under the contribution limits for C corporations). The rules for how these are allocated are the same as for S corporation ESOPs, and the use of an aggressive strategy to pay down a loan quickly with dividends raises the same have/have-not issues. There can also be a problem if the company's share value declines. The law requires that dividends release shares from the suspense account that have a value equal to the value of the dividends. If the share price has declined, there may not be enough shares, generally requiring the company to contribute make-up shares. But if the company is already at the annual contribution limit, that may not be possible. As with distributions, then, using dividends to repay a loan aggressively needs to be very carefully and cautiously considered.

Recycling Versus Redemption

As discussed above, companies can redeem shares (the company buys them back) or recycle them (the company buys them back and recontributes them, or the plan buys the shares from the company). The discussion about where the cash comes from covers many of the issues in recycling versus redemption, but there is also a more philosophical issue.

In the past, ESOPs were often set up to buy out one or more owner, but there was no intention of staying an ESOP in the long term. As employees left, the company redeemed the shares, winding down the ESOP and leaving one or more managers with control. Other companies planned to look for a buyer sometime after the ESOP paid off its debt. For these companies, redemption was the obvious choice.

Today, more and more companies want to become and stay 100% employee-owned. That means they want to make sure that new employees get shares and that non-ESOP owners are eventually bought out.

If they have non-ESOP owners who want to sell, the ESOP can buy their shares, and that may provide them with the ability to defer tax on the gain. The ESOP could pay no more than fair market value for their shares. Alternatively, the company can redeem the shares. There would be more flexibility in this process because the company could pay a premium. The board has to approve the transaction, and the board's fiduciary obligation requires it to determine that this premium does not constitute a waste of corporate assets. The ESOP trustee, as a shareholder, could sue the board for failing to make this determination. Still, some modest premium might be justifiable if the redemption brought the ESOP to 100% ownership and the company could become, if it were or converted to S status, non-taxable. In some case, the only way to get a remaining owner or owners to sell is to pay the premium.

In this case, when the shares are redeemed, all the ESOP participants would own a larger percentage of the company (because there are fewer shares). Their share value would not be affected if the redemption is for fair market value but would be if a premium were paid. The tax shield provided by S status cannot be incorporated into valuation, so even though the redemption makes good business sense in the long term, the short-term impact of a redemption at a premium price would be some decline in share value. Trustees must assess whether that is in the best interest of participants.

When ESOP participants sell their shares, again the company could buy them or the ESOP could (recycling the shares). Redemptions may be justified if the company has consistent and exceptionally high repurchase costs. That can happen if share prices rise quickly. Generally, redeeming the shares at fair market value should have a net neutral effect on the share price because the employees own a larger percentage of a now smaller company (in terms of its enterprise value). If the company instead recycles repurchased shares, and share price grows quickly, it might mean the required annual contributions to the ESOP to pay for the shares would be at a level that is economically unsustainable for the company. A downside of a redemption strategy is that could limit shares available to new employees. As noted elsewhere, however, it often makes sense, especially for 100% ESOP-owned S corporations, to redeem shares and then recontribute some or all of them over time on a consistent percentage-of-total-eligible pay basis.

With recycling, the company needs to contribute cash to the plan or use cash already in the plan to repurchase shares. New employees would get some of these shares. Two potential downsides are where the amount needed to be contributed annually becomes economically unsustainable and where the company has a very lumpy distribution pattern. In that case, in some years little gets recycled and in others a great deal, creating winners and losers in the ESOP based on what years individual employees happen to work there.

The Impact of Repurchase Obligations on Valuation

Until the late 1990s, the conventional wisdom on the repurchase obligation's effect on value was that it should not be a factor unless the appraiser judged that the company would not be able to fund it. To the extent it was considered, it was generally through the marketability discount.[2]

Most appraisers argued that the put option in an ESOP reduced or eliminated the marketability discount; others argued it depended on the plan's proven ability to repurchase shares. In either case, the discount for the repurchase obligation was usually very small, typically 5%. A few appraisers and some lawyers, on the other hand, contended that the put option is not the same thing as a liquid market and should provide only a small reduction in the marketability discount, meaning the shares might be discounted another 20% or more. Some went even further, arguing that the put option was a right of participants, not the plan, and the valuation was for the plan, meaning the full marketability discount should be used.

Outside of the marketability discount, however, very few appraisers contended that the cash flow implications of repurchase should affect valuation. The core of the argument was that the appraisal assumed a willing buyer. The willing buyer would extinguish the repurchase obligation when the stock was sold. Because a company could always choose to sell, no consideration of cash flow issues should be applied. In fact, to do so would mean participants would get stock at too low a price.

---

2. The marketability discount is based on how easy or hard it is for a participant to sell shares. Some appraisers argued that the more uncertainty there was about the company's ability to fund the repurchase in the future, the larger the discount should be. Often, this discount ranged from 5% to 15%.

As ESOPs matured, however, many companies faced a difficult scenario. Their cash needs to cover the repurchase obligation were often well in excess of what they would contribute to retirement plans if they did not have an ESOP. Appraisers, by ignoring that, were using future free cash flow projections that were unrealistically high. People who left sooner got a windfall; those who left later got a haircut. In the worst-case scenario, such as the Antioch case described at the beginning of this book, companies were forced to sell when they did not want to or went bankrupt. From a fiduciary standpoint, the company was sacrificing the long-term interests of the plan for the short-term benefit of some participants.

There was considerable debate on this issue, and it is still not resolved. The NCEO strongly endorsed the idea that repurchase obligations should factor into valuations, however, and so did a growing number of independent trustees. By the latter part of the first decade of the 2000s, this view became the norm among these trustees and was increasingly accepted by appraisers. NCEO surveys showed that more companies were asking appraisers about this issue and providing them with copies of repurchase analyses, although many companies were still ignoring it and some appraisers did not agree with the trustee position. In 2006, the Seventh Circuit Court of Appeals ruled in *Armstrong vs. LaSalle National Bank* that factoring in repurchase obligations was a clear ESOP fiduciary duty.

In our view at the NCEO, not factoring repurchase obligations into valuation is the single biggest threat to ESOP sustainability. But how should it be done? Several factors will play into the calculation, including:

- Distribution policies
- Vesting
- Eligibility
- Other repurchase obligations, such as for synthetic equity granted to executives
- How much the ESOP owns
- Demographics
- Company financial performance

- How much cash the ESOP has and is expected to have over time
- When the loan will be repaid
- Expected change in stock price
- Whether shares are redeemed or recycled

To perform the calculation, an appraiser might use one or more of these methods:

- *The expected contribution rate to the ESOP and other retirement plans relative to what the company would need to contribute to these plans to be competitive in the market:* For instance, if a company needs to put in an extra 7% of pay to fund an ESOP that buys back the shares, that contribution can be used to reduce the expected future earnings. For some companies, the ESOP contribution may be high relative to other companies, but a high level of contributions is an ongoing part of the company's employment philosophy that a competitor would have to pay as well to keep the current workforce. In that case, the calculation might be adjusted for this factor.
- *Projected working capital impact:* Companies that cannot meet repurchase needs out of normal cash flow or funds in the ESOP might need to maintain higher levels of working capital to assure the funds will be there when needed. A cyclical business, for instance, might particularly need to do this. Appraisers would then adjust the working capital's impact on the ultimate value.
- *Adjusting market multiples or marketability discounts:* The theory here is that the added obligation makes the pricing multiple (typically for EBITDA) lower because of uncertainties in meeting the obligation or can increase the marketability discount because the certainty of repurchases is less.

If the appraiser does determine a lower value than would be the case absent the repurchase obligation, that will in turn lower the obligation. The calculations thus need to be iterated enough times to reach a solution.

Should You Releverage Your ESOP to Fund Repurchases?

An idea that has gained some currency in recent years is to partly or entirely releverage an ESOP. There are many variations on this theme. The core idea is that the company purchases either ESOP-held shares or shares from terminated employees, and then the ESOP borrows money from the company to reacquire the shares.

In the most extreme scenario, the company buys back all the shares in the ESOP, terminates it or converts it to another plan, and sells the shares to a new leveraged ESOP. Say there are 100,000 shares at $100 per share, with a total value of $10 million. The company buys the 100,000 shares, borrowing the $10 million if needed. The shares are now owned by the company. ESOP participants now have $10 million in cash in their accounts rather than $10 million in shares. Because the plan no longer would qualify as an ESOP if the cash remained in employee accounts (because the ESOP would no longer be primarily invested in company stock), the money could either be paid out and the ESOP terminated, or the ESOP could be converted to a 401(k) or profit sharing plan. If the ESOP is terminated, everyone is vested and then receives the payout.

The second step is for the company to set up "ESOP 2." ESOP 2 borrows money to buy the shares back from the company. The shares are allocated as the loan is repaid. The effect of this is that all employees are at the ground floor of the new ESOP. Because of all the debt taken on to repurchase the shares, the enterprise value will be lower than before the debt was incurred.

Less dramatically, the company can borrow enough money to buy just some percentage of the shares in the plan, or shares from terminated employees. In this case, the plan would still be primarily invested in employer stock, so it would continue to operate, unlike the "ESOP 2" scenario above. This could be done in a number of ways:

1. The company could buy back all the shares from terminated employees who still have account balances, and then sell the shares back to the ESOP (financed by a loan from the company to the plan). That might make sense if a company has a very large repurchase obligation from this group compared to projections for active employees.

This most typically occurs in companies with a lot of people who reach retirement age at the same time.

2. The company could buy the same percentage of shares from all employee accounts. Employee accounts would get cash for the shares. The ESOP would then borrow funds to buy some or all of these shares back and reallocate them as the loan is repaid, thus getting shares to new employees in higher numbers than if this had not been done. The money the company uses to buy the shares from terminated employees is a nonproductive expense that will reduce enterprise value.

3. The company can make a one-time substantial diversification offer to all employees. The offer could provide that cash would actually be paid out to employees, or it could provide that the cash for the shares either remain in their ESOP account or be transferred to a 401(k) plan. The shares now would be held by the company. The ESOP could then borrow money to buy these shares back and reallocate them over time as the loan is repaid. If a company is performing well, however, it may find that not many people choose to diversify. Companies could combine this with the second approach above, however (buying shares from employee accounts, which the ESOP would then repurchase).

4. Finally, in any of these approaches, the company could redeem the shares and then recontribute them to the ESOP (whether ESOP 2 or the existing ESOP) on an annual, discretionary basis. This would mean new employees would be getting shares along with everyone else, but plan participants would not benefit from leveraging. In contrast, if the ESOP borrows money to buy a block of shares, the appreciation on all those shares, including in the suspense account, will get passed on to participants as the shares are released over time. If instead the company holds the shares and recontributes them year by year, the appreciation accrues to the company, assuming, as is normally the case, that the contribution is made based on a percentage-of-pay basis.[3]

---

3. To explain this further, assume that a company buys back 50,000 shares for $100 each, or $5 million. In the first case, the shares are held in suspense. Assume 10% are released each year. In year 2, the shares are now worth $107.

Any of these approaches only work for companies with very strong cash flows and/or available cash reserves.

Conclusion

A sustainable plan to address the repurchase obligation is essential to assure an ESOP is viable for the long term. Some people say that this obligation is a drawback of an ESOP, but it is well to remember that all private companies have a 100% repurchase obligation all the time. ESOPs just have it on a schedule in dribs and drabs rather than in occasional major events. A substantial repurchase obligation is also a sign of success. Companies that plan repurchases carefully will be able to manage their obligations and help all their owners thrive.

KEY TAKEAWAYS

- *Get the repurchase study right.* Work with professional advisors to set up an ongoing repurchase analysis at least every three years. Consider expected turnover and retirements, alternative stock price growth models, distribution policies, whether the stock is redeemed or recycled, and other factors the adviser considers essential.

- *Align corporate strategy with the repurchase obligation.* How aggressive do you want to be in using cash flow or reserves to grow, including by acquisitions? Make sure your approach is conservative enough to deal with unexpected downturns, but not so cautious that business opportunities to increase profits are avoided.

- *Determine whether the cash for repurchase comes from the company or contributions to the ESOP.* Generally, 100% ESOP-owned S corporations have little advantage to making contributions to the ESOP to buy back shares because there is no tax deduction for doing so. It is usually better to buy back the shares at the corporate level then

---

Now employees get 5,000 shares worth $107 each instead of $100 each. In the nonleveraged example, the company recontributes enough shares to meet some target percentage of pay. If the share value goes up, the company needs to contribute fewer shares. All this match will make more difference if there are non-ESOP owners, of course. If the company is 100% ESOP-owned, the employees ultimately still get the value of the appreciation.

recontribute them as needed to meet a stable compensation strategy. Other ESOPs may want to fund repurchases with contributions, but if they have a "lumpy" distribution pattern they may want to buy back shares at the corporate level then recontribute (and deduct) share contributions to the ESOP on a more level basis.

- *Decide whether you should recycle or redeem shares.* If you want to sustain the ESOP in the long term, shares need to go back into the ESOP one way or another. An aggressive redemption strategy is mostly used as a way to wind down the ESOP.
- *Make sure appraisals reflect the repurchase obligation.* If your appraisal does not factor repurchase costs into projected cash flow, discounts for lack of liquidity, capitalization rates, or some other key metric, you may end up overpaying for shares in the short term and creating a potential cash crunch. Only plans that have substantial cash reserves, usually in the ESOP, can ignore the interaction of repurchase and value.
- *Should you refinance the ESOP?* Companies whose stock price is growing quickly, that have a large repurchase obligation, and have either strong cash flow or reserves may want to consider having the ESOP borrow money to buy back shares from employees who are getting distributions or possibly buy back a substantial part of the ESOP's existing holdings and then allocate the purchased shares over time to ESOP accounts. This approach can help solve the have/have not problem and delay the repurchase obligation, but raises fiduciary issues that need careful consideration.

Chapter 4

Valuation Issues

As the Antioch example that started this books shows, not managing the appraisal process effectively can make it difficult or impossible to sustain an ESOP for the long term. This chapter looks at three key issues in that process: making sure you comply with emerging best practices to reduce the threat of litigation and audit settlements, factoring in the repurchase obligation in the appraisal, and knowing what to do when fiduciaries suspect the appraisal firm is not doing a good job.

Best Practices for Fiduciaries in Valuation Oversight

In 2014, the Department of Labor (DOL) and GreatBanc Trust came to a settlement in a valuation lawsuit. The settlement included an agreement between GreatBanc and the DOL on best practices for overseeing the valuation process. While these only apply to GreatBanc, they set out a series of procedures that fiduciaries can use as guidelines for how to oversee the appraisal process in a prudent manner.[1]

The agreement states that trustees first must "prudently investigate the valuation advisor's qualifications" and take "reasonable steps to determine that the valuation advisor receives complete, accurate, and current information necessary to value the employer securities." The trustee also must determine "that its reliance on the valuation advisor's advice is reasonable before entering into any transaction in reliance on the advice." The appraiser should not have valued the stock that is to be the subject of the transaction with the ESOP for a party to the transaction other than the trustee. This last issue is controversial, however. If

---

1. For a detailed analysis, including the text of the agreement itself, see Theodore M. Becker, Bradford P. Campbell, and Julie A. Govreau, *The DOL Fiduciary Process Agreement for ESOP Transactions* (NCEO, 2014) (see nceo.org/r/agreement).

a company hires ABC Appraisers to do a preliminary valuation before deciding to do an ESOP or ABC has valued the company for other reasons in the past, it would seem to make sense to retain them for the ESOP valuation if they are qualified in ESOP appraisals and the trustee believes they meet the necessary standards. After all, they have already become familiar with the company. Many advisors do not believe they should be precluded, provided they do no other work for the company.

Trustees need to document why they chose the appraiser and how they vetted the appraiser's qualifications. This need not be done every time for appraisers used regularly. The trustee should know the qualifications of the person actually doing the work, not just the firm.

The agreement does not provide guidance on how to assure the appraiser is qualified, but some of the things that can be considered are reviewing a sample appraisal report from the provider (they should be able to do this with names blacked out), seeing if the appraiser has written for professional publications and/or spoken at conferences, and can provide a client list to call for references. If the firm's clients have been subject to litigation or DOL compliance procedures concerning audits, it should be able to explain the results satisfactorily.

One of the more important parts of the agreement concerns the specific documentation a valuation firm should obtain from the company. These include looking at a number of specific metrics on projected financial performance and how they compare over the prior five-year prior period as well as to comparable public company data, if any. The measurements described in the agreement are fairly standard in good ESOP appraisals; the agreement specifies what to look for and document.

The agreement also provides that the appraiser's report or trustee's documentation should demonstrate consideration of how "plan document provisions regarding stock distributions, the duration of the ESOP loan, and the age and tenure of the ESOP participants may affect the ESOP sponsor's prospective repurchase obligation, the prudence of the stock purchase, or the fair market value of the stock." This underscores an emerging but not yet universal practice of considering repurchase obligations and other distribution issues in connection with the appraisal.

The agreement requires that the trustee evaluate the debt for the transaction and the company's ability to repay it. It also requires that the trustee consider the fairness of the transaction with respect to such issues as whether the cost of the debt is reasonable.

The agreement states a clear preference for audited company financial statements in connection with the appraisal. If the company's financial statements are not audited, the trustee needs to document why it is reasonable to rely on unaudited financial information. Many ESOP companies do rely on statements that are reviewed instead of audited; if your company does this, your trustees need to document why this is appropriate.

The agreement prescribes that the trustee should document that any information, including financial projections, provided to the appraiser is reasonable. The trustee should also document that it has considered a list of 16 different items in the valuation report, including assumptions as to various discounts, adjustments to financial projections made by the appraiser, the weighting of various methods of appraisal, discount rates, the treatment of debt, the assessment of the company relative to markets and the industry, and other standard elements of ESOP appraisals.

The trustee also should document the specific steps taken to assess the valuation report as well as who did the work. That should include a discussion of the questions asked and areas of disagreement and how they were resolved.

The agreement also provides that "the trustee will consider whether it is appropriate to request a claw-back arrangement or other purchase price adjustment(s) to protect the ESOP against the possibility of adverse consequences in the event of significant corporate events or changed circumstances." A "claw-back" generally requires that the seller returns some of the price he or she received for stock sold in the event that the value of the stock goes down significantly during a specific period of time after the transaction. It is difficult to get a seller to agree to such a provision, but the agreement states that the trustee should document in writing their consideration of the appropriateness of a "claw-back or other purchase price adjustment(s)."

The agreement generally does not break new ground in what is generally seen as prudent processes in evaluating and acting on an ESOP appraisal in connection with a transaction. That should provide some comfort to ESOP practitioners and companies in that the DOL is not setting out new and potentially difficult criteria for ESOP appraisals.

This agreement is important because it lays out a specific process that trustees should follow in showing that they have proceeded appropriately in concluding that the ESOP is not paying more than fair market value for its shares. Trustees who follow these steps may have a greater degree of confidence that the appraisal process will not be challenged.

Factoring in the Repurchase Obligation

Until the late 1990s, the general assumption of the valuation community was that the repurchase obligation should not be considered in determining value. The argument is twofold. First, if the company were sold to an outside buyer, even a financial buyer, the repurchase obligation would go away. Lowering a company's fair market value assessment to reflect repurchase obligations would therefore mean the ESOP would be paying less than what a willing buyer would pay. Second, because the company could always put itself up for sale if it did not have the liquidity to handle repurchases, there was no need to consider this growing cash obligation in the same way other emerging financial obligations would be treated.

The second argument (the company could always put itself up for sale) is not persuasive. If a company reaches a point where it cannot handle its repurchase obligation and is forced to sell, it may put itself on the market at precisely the wrong time to get a good price. The first argument, though, is more serious. Some attorneys argued, and a few still do, that not paying departing employees what a potential buyer would pay violates ERISA by paying those employees less than fair market value. This view has been largely trumped, however, by concerns that paying people out at a price that does not factor in repurchases means people who leave early get paid a premium while those who leave later get a lower price. The Department of Labor, in the GreatBanc settlement discussed at the beginning of this chapter, agrees.

The argument here is straightforward. Emerging repurchase obligations represent nonproductive claims on future cash flows and/or existing cash reserves. In some ESOP companies, there may be ample resources to pay these claims, as explained below. In others, the claims require contributions to the ESOP no greater than what a company would otherwise contribute to retirement plans of one kind or another.

Most ESOP companies, however, find that to fund this obligation, they need to make cash contributions to the ESOP, and/or repurchase shares at the company level, in amounts that exceed normal retirement benefit costs. Other things being equal, that should reduce projected future earnings.

Assume XYZ Company has performed a repurchase obligation study and projects it will need to pay $2 million to former participants in the next four years. The company is 100% owned by the ESOP and has paid off all its acquisition debt. The ESOP has $200,000 in cash it can use for repurchases. The ESOP trustee's appraisal firm has indicated that normal retirement plan contributions for a company of its size in its industry come to 4% of eligible pay. To provide the additional $1.8 million, however, it will need the equivalent of 8% of pay each year. This might be contributed directly to the ESOP to use to repurchase shares, or some or all of the shares of departing participants can be repurchased by the company, and the shares can either be retired or recontributed (most ESOP companies will recontribute the shares, although they may smooth out the contributions to have a consistent annual contribution level). This additional 4% of pay represents an additional burden on cash flow. When calculating projected future earnings, therefore, this amount should not be included.

It may be, of course, that the company has cash reserves for the purpose of funding the repurchase obligation. While this changes the specific calculations used in appraisals, reducing available cash reserves obviously would normally produce a lower value.

This is a simplified conceptual model. Appraisers may use this approach or some other method to calculate the effect of repurchases, sometimes adjusting a liquidity discount, sometimes changing the discount rate used on projected future earnings to reflect repurchase risks, or some other approach. ESOP trustees need to be comfortable that the methodology is appropriate.

Some companies, however, may find that the repurchase obligation is not a factor because the ESOP has a lot of cash. The most common reason for this is that an ESOP was set up in an S corporation and did not own 100% of the shares. As distributions were made to non-ESOP owners to pay taxes, the ESOP got pro-rata distributions, building up cash. Other ESOP companies may, for various reasons, periodically contribute cash to the ESOP. In effect, these companies have already reduced their earnings from what they might have been had they not made these contributions.

Factoring in repurchases will lower the fair market value run of the valuation model. But now that it has been lowered, the repurchase obligation will go down. So the calculations must be repeated ("iterated" in appraisal terminology) until a mathematical solution is found.

So why is factoring in repurchases so important, and how can it be justified from a fiduciary standpoint? Fiduciaries are charged with the duty to maximize the long-term value of plan assets. If employees in one year are overpaid for their shares because the cash flow or reserve account implications of the repurchase obligation are not taken into consideration, the employees in later years will get less. In some cases, the impact may be great enough to force a sale even if the market is not opportune or, more likely, impair the company's long-term ability to use cash to grow. For all these reasons, almost all institutional ESOP trustees now require that valuations consider the repurchase obligation.

There are non-fiduciary issues as well. Many ESOP companies want to stay employee-owned for the very long term. Unless they manage and control their repurchase obligations, this will not be possible.

Trustees should provide appraisers with a repurchase assessment on a regular basis. Ideally, the company will have a formal repurchase study done at least every few years. The company may do an internal update of the projections annually or indicate in a more general way if expected obligations are expected to go up or down.

What Happens If You Decide Your Appraiser Is Not Doing a Good Job?

Occasionally, a fiduciary may decide that the current appraisal is not reliable. It may be, for instance, that the appraiser is not using generally accepted assumptions about various discounts for liquidity or control, not factoring in repurchase obligations in an acceptable way, or applying inappropriate multiples or discount rates.

The best strategy in these situations is to hire a qualified ESOP appraisal firm to review the valuation. Ideally, the engagement letter should specify that the reviewing firm will not be hired to do a new appraisal, but there may be compelling reasons to make the reviewing firm the first choice. At the very least, the engagement letter should specify that the reviewing firm may not be hired to do a new appraisal if one is deemed needed.

The review is not a new appraisal. Instead, the reviewing firm will read the report to look for potential methodological errors. The fiduciaries then must decide whether to engage a new firm or raise the issues with the existing appraiser. The existing appraiser may be able to satisfactorily answer any concerns or may agree to change certain assumptions, in which case that firm would continue to do the work. If the fiduciary is not satisfied, then a new appraiser should be hired.

Getting more than one appraisal and choosing the best is not a good option. If the two results disagree, how should one be chosen? The result could look like appraisal-shopping, which is never a good idea should fiduciaries be challenged.

Conclusion

Inappropriate valuation methodologies and fiduciary review processes are among the most serious threats to the long-term viability of an ESOP. Those responsible for overseeing the process need to adhere to the highest standards of care.

KEY TAKEAWAYS

- *Get your procedures in order:* The GreatBanc settlement agreement is important to read and consider. Most ESOP advisors agree that trustees do not necessarily need to do everything the settlement specifies, but trustees should have a well-documented procedure for how they choose appraisers and assess the valuation process.

- *Factor in the repurchase obligation:* Every ESOP company needs to do periodic repurchase analyses and make sure appraisers are weighing the financial implications of these projections in their conclusions of value.

- *If you don't think your appraisal is sound, get an outside review.* Hire an independent appraiser to assess the approach and process of your valuation. They should not do a new appraisal.

Chapter 5

Leadership Succession and ESOP Sustainability

Sam Haines was the president of Gear Motions, a successful manufacturer of custom gears in Syracuse, New York. In 2001, Sam hired a strong number two person as VP and CFO who he hoped would eventually be his successor. The new hire helped set up an ESOP to buy 36% of the stock from the owners, all in the Haines family. While the new hire was very enthused about the ESOP and seemed a great fit, by 2006, he realized he really did not want to be the president. A new person was brought in, but she did not work out either and left after 18 months. Finally, a third successor came in and worked out very well. Haines says, "the takeaway here is that in a small (under $20 million) manufacturing company, fit [especially in an ESOP] is as important as skill, so one really needs to start succession planning early."

But the transition really was not complete. Outside board members were added in 2010, two thirds of whom are from growing ESOP companies. Haines now feels the transition process is complete, leaving the company with good leadership and a strong, 100% ESOP.

Things do not always work out so well, however. Robert Beyster built Science Applications International Corporation into an exceptionally successful company, one deeply committed to the idea of being employee-owned through an ESOP, stock purchases, stock options, and other means. He diluted his own ownership over the years to help spread ownership widely while creating a truly engaged, high-involvement culture. The company grew from a handful of employees to over 40,000. But when Beyster was ready to retire, there was no logical internal successor to replace him. So the board looked to outsiders. All the finalists were asked how they felt about employee ownership as a core company value. Of course, they were all smart enough to say how important they thought it was. The new CEO, however, was not as committed as he said. In relatively short order, the company went public, employee ownership was deemphasized, and more traditional management approaches instituted. CEOs came and went in quick succession; the company's stock price moved mostly sideways. Ultimately, it split into two companies. Beyster felt deeply discouraged.

Leadership in any company is a challenge, but it is even more difficult in an employee ownership company. The new leader needs to not only lead the company in all the usual ways but also honor and grow the ownership culture. This may be at odds with traditional views about what makes a good CEO or president. Great leaders, like Jack Stack at SRC Holdings, are highly capable, innovative, efficient, and visionary, but they are also humble. Stack built the remarkably successful culture at SRC (now famous as the Great Game of Business) on the assumption that neither he nor any of the other managers at the company knew best just because they were managers. He genuinely believed—and convinced other people he believed—that the janitor, the machine operator, the receptionist—anyone—could have a great idea no one else may have thought about. It is that kind of humility that creates the opening for truly participative employee cultures. As this book's chapter on ownership culture discusses, what really makes employee ownership work well is the ability for lots of people at all levels to generate and act on ideas. But many people who rise to the top do so because they have great ideas and drive—and often come to believe (in part because everyone tells them) just how unique their talents are.

Succession is not just about CEO's successor, however. There are leaders at all levels of a company. Many are managers, but others may have special technical skills, may head ESOP communication committees, may be colleagues other employees look to for guidance, and so on. It is important to be able to replace these people effectively as well. This chapter discusses two companies that do this exceptionally well.

Finally, as Sam Haines pointed out, leadership transition also often means adding outside board members who can help the company grow and bring new perspectives to management. Board issues are discussed in this book's chapter on governance.

Identifying and Integrating the New CEO

Finding a new CEO (for the sake of simplicity, we'll call whoever is designated as the top corporate officer the CEO) can be a challenging task, especially in closely held companies where the current top leader may have started the company and/or been in that role for many years, often decades. Employees, customers, board members, and suppliers have all become accustomed to the way the old CEO works. Change can be difficult, and the new CEO may face the challenge of these various constituencies wishing that the new CEO would do this or that the way the old CEO did. If the old CEO is around, they may even tell him or her what they don't like about the new leader, creating an awkward situation all around.

The first question to address is whether to hire an insider or an outsider. The research on succession planning is unfortunately almost entirely limited to public companies. CEOs in these companies typically have fairly short tenure (an average of about five years) and are subject to very different pressures than CEOs of closely held companies. The research on public companies does generally find that internal successors do better than external ones. One of the largest studies was a 2009 analysis by Booz Allen that found that from 2009 to 2011, insiders outperformed their regional stock market index by a median 4.4%, while outsider CEOs delivered 0.5% shareholder return. Jim Collins, author of *Good to Great,* strongly endorses the insider successor argument, noting that almost all the companies he has looked at that persisted over time and became "great" used insider successors.

Joseph Boyer, a professor at the Harvard Business School, notes in the November 2007 issue of the *Harvard Business Review* that while the research does show that outside successors have a much higher risk of failing, "both insider and outsider CEOs have strengths and weaknesses when they begin. Insiders know the company and its people but are often blind to the need for radical change—they've drunk the Kool-Aid. Outsiders see the need for a new approach but can't foster change because they don't know the company or industry sector well enough."

In fact, there are lots of pros and cons to insiders versus outsiders. Outsiders may:

- Bring in new perspectives and/or energy. When companies have long-term CEOs, they can become very insular and resistant to change. That is especially true in companies that are successful. It is easy to overlearn from success and just keep doing the same things until they fail. The best advice I ever got on my own succession at the NCEO was not to expect—or look for—a clone but rather to find someone who did some things the same, some things differently, some things worse, and some things better.

- Have skills and experience that current insiders lack.
- Have connections to other business leaders and market opportunities that can open new doors.
- Adapt poorly to a high-involvement, open-book management culture—these are not common outside of employee-owned companies.
- Be resented by those insiders who believe they should have gotten the job.
- Have great business skills, but not necessarily in your particular business.
- Take a year or two to learn what they need to know about the new business they head.

Insiders have their own pros and cons:

- Presumably, they will be selected in part because of their cultural fit.
- They may be more readily accepted by employees generally, who often fear the change that an outsider might bring.
- They may be less aware of or open to charting new courses.
- They will take much less time to get up to speed on what they need to do in their new role.
- They may be selected because they are insiders and make the selection process easier—even if they are not really the best fit.

Boyer's great insight, I think, is that a succession process for a new CEO can aim for the best of both. From early on, potential successors need to be identified (or hired) based not just on their skills and experience, but also their willingness to challenge existing conventional wisdom in productive ways. Ideal candidates should be open to new ideas from both inside and outside the firm. That means existing CEOs need to be able to tolerate disagreement and recognize their own limitations.

A few case studies will illustrate the process various ESOP companies have used to identify new CEOs and get them ready to assume their new job. The companies profiled below show three approaches: pure insider succession, bringing in an outsider but not promoting that person to CEO for several years, and hiring an outsider.

Barclay Water Management

I sit on the board of directors of Barclay Water Management, an 85-employee Watertown, Massachusetts, provider of water treatment services for boiler operations and water hygiene. Its ESOP owns a minority of the shares, but by 2017 should own 100% of the shares. Its current CEO when this was written (2015), Bill Brett, has been the CEO since 1973 and has led the company to consistent profits and workplace awards. He is widely respected in the industry and by employees. In 2014, Brett announced that he would be stepping down in the next two to three years.

As one of the outside board members at Barclay, I knew it would be a challenge to replace Bill. The board, which has one other outsider, strongly agreed that an insider would be best, but we were open to looking outside the company as well. As a first step, we asked Bill to identify a few possible candidates. We knew each of these fairly well from our interactions with them over the years. But more important, we wanted to know what employees thought about succession. So we arranged to have a series of in-depth interviews with several employees from all walks of the company at the January 2015 annual meeting.

In discussions, we asked each employee what he or she thought about the leadership succession issue. Should it be an insider or outsider? Were there any existing insiders they thought should be the new CEO? What were they looking for in a new CEO? What were the pros and cons of whomever they identified?

We found an extremely strong preference for not hiring from the outside. Barclay employees are very loyal to the company and its culture. That culture has evolved in the last few years to generate a lot more employee participation in creating new ideas, processes, and services, leading to record profits even in the face of often difficult industry conditions. They were skeptical that any outsider would honor that culture enough.

They also all identified similar traits they wanted in a new CEO, such as openness to new ideas, strong sales skills and experience (about half the workforce is in sales), demonstrated effectiveness, and respect from other employees. All but one person named the current CFO as the best choice; the one who did not named two people, one of whom was the current sales manager. Bill also thought the current sales manager was the right choice.

We also asked employees to identify rising younger leaders. Here too there was essentially unanimous consent that one of the young sales managers was a potential star. This person can now start being groomed for a higher leadership role, maybe even eventually becoming the new CEO when the next one retires, probably in the next ten years or so.

Windings

Windings is a 100% ESOP-owned custom manufacturer. In 2000, long before his retirement, CEO Roger Ryberg began planning a management transition. He recruited Jerry Kauffman, who was working at a larger company. "When I was looking for a successor, I wanted to find someone with character, integrity, and a certain way of interacting with people," said Ryberg. "I also wanted to take at least five years to see how he fit at Windings. I made sure Jerry knew I was committed to the ESOP. I gave him challenges and then just got out of the way to see how he would handle them." Kauffman joined Windings partly because he wanted to work for a smaller company, and having an equity stake was important to him. "The basic values that Roger and Windings exemplified were the most important reason I decided to join the company," he said. Those values are evident in the way Kauffman described his goals as CEO, a position he assumed in 2009. "I can give someone the opportunity to have satisfaction in their job by tapping into their intrinsic motivation to do something good in the world."

Kauffman is an example of a well-developed outside-in strategy. After being hired as an outsider in 2000, there was a long glide path to become the new CEO—if indeed the board decided that he was the right person. This gave Windings time both to fully assess him and prepare him for his new role.

Central States Manufacturing

Other ESOPs have decided outsiders were necessary. In the NCEO publication *Moving On: Making the Transition After Selling to an ESOP*,[1] Rick Carpenter of Central States Manufacturing, a 100% ESOP-owned company in Arkansas, writes:

> As a company we did not do well in developing internal candidates for the CEO position. When I decided to step down as CEO, we decided to use a search firm.
>
> In addition to using a CEO recruiting firm, we also used a corporate psychologist to help vet the candidates. The corporate psychologist specialized in evaluating CEOs. She has interviewed and tested over 100 CEO candidates. She developed a database of these candidates and followed up on their performance. Using these data and analyses, she developed personality testing to evaluate the capabilities and fit of a candidate to fill a CEO role, a process that worked very well. We hired our candidate during the summer of 2013.

The process at Central States went well beyond what a typical headhunter would do. The decision to focus on personality issues is not a common one—but perhaps it should be. Carpenter, however, has stayed on as chairman of the board, which also has a number of impressively qualified outsiders. His main role now is to work with the CEO and others to maintain Central States' strong open-book management, high-involvement culture.

Dealey Renton and Associates

Dealey Renton and Associates (DRA) is a 100% ESOP-owned insurance agency in Oakland, California, with a particular focus on engineering and architecture. It has been ESOP owned since the 1970s and has been consistently profitable. In 2012, its board started to encourage its longtime CEO, Al Chinn, to think about when he wanted to retire and who might replace him. At that time, Chinn was not sure when that would be, but he was reaching a point in his life when the challenges of running a business, particularly in the severe recession in the architecture

---

1. Corey Rosen, Christopher J. Clarkson, and Stacie Jacobsen, *Moving On: Making the Transition After Selling to an ESOP* (NCEO, 2015) (see nceo.org/r/moving).

and engineering field in California from 2008 to 2013, made staying well past normal retirement age unappealing (he was in his early 60s).

The board and Chinn decided there really were no internal candidates for succession. Partly because DRA was such a good employer and so stable, it has a large number of very senior people. While some of them might have the skills to be the new CEO, they too were at or near retirement age. In fact, one of the challenges for the new CEO would be recruiting new talent.

Chinn was very well connected in the insurance business and knew people in a lot of other companies well enough to have some sense of who might be a good fit. One, Morgan West, was a particularly promising candidate. West was a charismatic and energetic executive at a Seattle company. He expressed not just a strong commitment to DRA's culture, but a desire to expand opportunities for employees to be more entrepreneurial. Over the next few months, Chinn and West had a number of meetings, eventually leading to a meeting with the board. The board was also very impressed, as was the ESOP trust committee, which at DRA is made up of several employees. The unusual trust committee structure at DRA allowed for broader and more representative input on West.

West was offered a job as vice president with the understanding that in the next two to three years, he would be the leading candidate to become CEO. That gave the board and employees enough time to get a better sense of his fit. In 2014, the board decided that he was the right candidate, and in 2015, Chinn announced that he would step down. During the two-year transition, West gradually took over the leadership role of the company, particularly in 2014. A number of productive changes have been made, and business is improving. Now West will face the difficult challenge of an industry that is rapidly consolidating, with many companies looking to buy agencies at exceptionally high multiples.

Leadership Succession Below the CEO Level

As critical as CEO succession is, successful companies need to replace leaders and people with critical skills at all levels. The best companies have formal programs for identifying and training new leaders. This process typically has several steps:

- Each person in a leadership position or with critical skills identifies what the essential abilities are for that position.
- Each person in a leadership position or with critical skills identifies what the best ways would be for a candidate to learn the needed skills the candidate does not currently possess.
- The company develops a training program on leadership development. This may be in-house with existing personnel, such as through mentoring, or it may be through bringing in outside trainers and/or sending candidates to various programs at trade associations, conferences, or colleges.
- Companies may ask potential new leaders to take on the kinds of projects they might lead in the future to test their skills.
- Companies may develop teams of potential leaders from their own learning groups to focus on developing skills.
- Some companies use various forms of personality assessments to help identify people who would be good fits for moving up.
- Some companies use job rotation programs to help people find the best fit for them.

This may seem like a daunting task and a lot of time, and many companies will do this more informally. That may work well, but companies need to realistically assess how well it is working and move to a more formal process as needed.

The best way to illustrate these ideas is to focus on two companies that do a particularly good job at this kind of organization-wide leadership succession, BL Companies and SRC Holdings.

BL Companies: Developing Current and Future Key Leaders

In our issue brief *Leadership Development and Succession in Employee-Owned Companies*,[2] Edmund Freeman described the highly successful process for leadership development BL Companies uses. This section is based on his essay.

---

2. Keith Boatright et al., *Leadership Development and Succession in Employee-Owned Companies* (NCEO, 2012) (see nceo.org/r/leadership).

BL Companies provides integrated architecture, engineering, and land surveying services to clients in the Northeast. It became 70% employee-owned in 2006 and 100% in 2010. It has about 160 employees. In 2007, it started a formal leadership assessment and development program. As a first step, senior executives created a competency model for all leadership positions. Eight core leadership qualities were identified:

- Teamwork
- Accountability
- Developing others
- Relationship-building
- Client focus
- Communications
- Strategic thinking
- Leading and managing change

In the next few years, BL rolled out a leadership development program for all levels of the company. It started with the HR process, where the new hires were assessed based in this competency model. How well they performed on these competencies was a key element in employee assessments.

The BL Leadership Foundations program provides a two-day program focusing on goal setting and development and how effectively people interacted with other employees. Employees were given emotional intelligence self-assessment tests, sat through a series of brief lectures, and held a number of discussions. The program started with 15 senior leaders, then cascaded to 12 other senior leaders, and finally down to 35 other employees, with people at each level taking responsibility for the next level. For the 12 most senior leaders, a series of three-day meetings was held to focus on core competency issues and discuss ways to be more effective leaders.

Next, employees were assigned to a cohort group. Participation was voluntary, but most people participated. Meetings were held monthly to discuss books and talk about progress on action plans and about how they were all doing on the core competency issues. There were also one-on-one mentoring programs between senior leaders and select employees.

Table 5-1, taken directly from Freeman's essay, provides details on the competency model.

Table 5-1	
Competencies	Behaviors Reflecting Competence
1 Accountability	Takes responsibility for one's own success
	Takes responsibility for the success of the team
	Takes responsibility for the decisions and success of the organization as a whole
	Makes timely decisions with best available knowledge
	Drives plans to closure
	Holds direct reports accountable for their responsibilities
	Holds cross-functional team members accountable for their responsibilities
2 Teamwork	Creates an atmosphere of shared purpose and shared accountability within the work team
	Creates an atmosphere of shared purpose and shared accountability across disciplines
	Promotes mutual understanding, mutual respect, enthusiasm, and performance within the work team
	Promotes mutual understanding, mutual respect, enthusiasm, and performance across disciplines
	Affirms the value of each team member
	Affirms the value of the whole team
	Affirms the value of leadership
	Initiates and embraces partnerships across the company and with clients to generate improved business outcomes
	Looks for true win-win solutions
	Promotes culture of shared ownership and shared rewards

Table 5-1

	Competencies	Behaviors Reflecting Competence
3	Developing Others	Understands where direct reports are in their professional development
		Works closely with direct reports to create realistic professional development plans
		Takes action to facilitate direct reports' professional development
		Promotes continuous improvement of the individual and the team by creating an environment that encourages taking on new challenges
		Sets high standards
		Creates a climate that helps bring about the best in others
		Communicates expected outcomes clearly and then lets people figure out how to get there
		Provides useful feedback
		Celebrates the successes of others
		Treats others' mistakes as learning opportunities
		Sets a good example for others to follow
4	Relationship Building	Invests the time to actively pursue and maintain relationships with employees to gain and maintain their trust and respect
		Invests the time to actively pursue and maintain relationships with clients to gain and maintain their trust and respect
		Invests the time to actively pursue and maintain relationships with external business partners (vendors, developers, brokers, agencies, etc.) to gain and maintain their trust and respect
		Shows consistency among principles, practices and behavior
		Understands and responds to the core goals, needs, and drivers of employees
		Understands and responds to the core goals, needs, and drivers of external business partners (vendors, developers, brokers, agencies, etc.)
		Follows through on commitments
		Treats everyone respectfully, regardless of position or role

Table 5-1

	Competencies	Behaviors Reflecting Competence
5	Client Focus	Demonstrates an understanding that "clients" include not only paying customers but also regulators, internal clients, and external business partners (vendors, developers, brokers, agencies, etc.)
		Identifies and understands clients' goals, needs, drivers and constraints
		Demonstrates an understanding that BL's success can only be achieved through superior client service
		Embraces quality as an essential attribute of all deliverables
		Develops individual and team expertise necessary to succeed in a chosen marketplace
		Projects value, knowledge, and expertise in the marketplace
		Develops and shares client relationships and leads to expand BL's network of connections and opportunities
6	Communication	Listens, asks questions, pays close attention, and seeks to understand others' verbal and nonverbal communications
		Tailors communications to the appropriate audience and the goal
		Expresses ideas clearly, concisely, and with impact
		Ensures all critical data, decisions, and commitments are appropriately documented
		Demonstrates confidence, "presence," and expertise in public speaking and other presentations
		Shares information appropriately among stakeholders

Table 5-1

	Competencies	Behaviors Reflecting Competence
7	Strategic Thinking	Identifies and prioritizes critical issues
		Establishes a clear vision of an outcome, then defines and acts upon tasks to achieve the outcome
		Considers financial impacts and implications when approaching challenges, opportunities, or issues
		Identifies, prioritizes, and acts on strategic issues while maintaining day-to-day responsibilities
		Understands and communicates how individual tasks and/or projects fit into the strategic direction of the firm
		Recognizes and drives innovations and/or technologies that will achieve competitive breakthroughs
		Understands the strengths and weaknesses of BL's competitors and positions BL accordingly with clients, prospects, and employees
8	Leading and Managing Change	Understands and provides a clear rationale and context regarding the need for change
		Provides a direction/vision that generates people's commitment
		Provides a clear sense of what needs to be done to move from the current reality to the future vision
		Teaches and models new behaviors by example
		Uses participative processes to gain people's buy-in to and ownership of change
		Empowers others to act by removing obstacles and resistance to change

SRC Holding: Leadership Development at All Levels

The most comprehensive leadership development program we at the NCEO know of comes from SRC Holdings. SRC is a 1,200-employee remanufacturer of engines in Springfield, Missouri (it was once called Springfield ReManufacturing). Bought by employees in 1983 when it was a 119-employee failing division of International Harvester, it has seen its stock price grow from 10 cents a share to over $360 today, while its work force has grown to 1,200. It has created multiple enterprises, some of which have been spun off.

From the outset, CEO Jack Stack wanted to create an exceptionally transparent company. He called the model he developed the Great Game of Business. All employees were taught to read and understand income statements and balance sheets. All employees participated in weekly or biweekly meetings, called huddles, to project critical numbers for their operations (backlog, waste, on-time delivery, margins, etc.) and assess how they were doing against prior projections. Employees use these numbers to meet in teams to develop new ideas and processes. The teams send representatives to cascade upward to company-wide huddles. Stack's insight was that if people were given the tools to understand and use the numbers, and the latitude to make decisions about how to improve them, everyone would think and act like a business person. The idea was so successful SRC created a new business division, The Great Game of Business, to teach people how to follow the model. Today, many ESOP companies have adopted it. Stack's book *The Great Game of Business* became a business bestseller, still in print over 20 years after it was first published.

In 2013, Keith Boatright, the human resources director at SRC, wrote a detailed article for the publication *Leadership Development and Succession in Employee-Owned Companies* (referred to above) on the SRC leadership development model, which I have excerpted and abridged below.

> At SRC Holdings, we see our succession management program as one of our most important strategic advantages. It is also one of our most important challenges because our managers must be good at not only their jobs but also building and maintaining our culture. That culture focuses intently on cultural training and communication at all levels of the organization. Involvement does not stop at the work level; it cascades up through high-involvement planning.
>
> Part of our core culture is that we want to provide employees paths for their own development. We believe this is part of our responsibility to our employee-owners, but it also helps us to build a pool of people who can be recruited for succession openings as they occur. With a business that is always growing and changing, it is important to have a process to continually strengthen and maintain our unique culture. Our succession planning process is the linchpin to achieving those goals.
>
> *The Basic Structure of Succession Planning*
> Our succession planning process relies on Jack Stack's belief that we need to develop people who think and act like owners, with an emphasis on talent

development, change management, relationship-building, and strategic thinking. To ensure that the process is consistent and ongoing, we formally revisit all succession plans in January and July each year.

Each January, the whole HR team meets with division general managers and company executive vice presidents. We conduct succession planning and skills competency reviews, identify and discuss talent, collaborate on the future direction of company's organizational structure, and assess human capital readiness to achieve our sales and marketing plan.

During this process, we rely on organizational charts that offer a snapshot of where each division of SRC is and where it is going. We then build off of that information to understand how the company will look when aligned with our five-year sales and marketing plans and make note of how we plan to add, modify, or omit positions as we grow. Throughout the year, we monitor the candidates' progress and continually reevaluate their readiness as a succession candidate.

In the next stage, we dive deeply into our workforce and employment data to evaluate succession planning results while actively supporting progress and alignment of our strategic workforce goals. During this process, the big objective is to complete detailed strategic workforce planning. In addition, we also revisit the individual development plans for a brief review. The goals of the July process can be achieved by answering four basic questions: Where are we going? What we will need to get there? Who do we have now? What are our talent gaps?

Steps to a Successful Succession Planning Program

To make the process work, we have learned that the first step is for top management to actively support integrating the strategy of managing the people process. Lots of companies pay lip service to this idea, but they often delegate it to HR and give HR limited authority, time, and money to create a thorough process. Top management involvement also sends a message that this is an essential part of their job, not just something to figure out when an opening appears.

Second, companies need a continuous process. Succession planning needs to be going on all the time, even if people think that a need may not arise soon. Moreover, the process at SRC involves employees at varying levels of the company, not just a few managers. The high-involvement nature of this planning helps make sure we are getting all the information and perspectives we need.

Third, companies need to define reality. Much of the process at SRC is to constantly rethink where we are in every business unit at every level. It is not something we do once in a while or when the need occurs, but on a regular, scheduled basis.

Fourth, at SRC we have developed extensive analytics to guide us. These tools are mostly numbers-based charts tracking individual development plans, needs, opportunities, strengths, weaknesses, and challenges, both internally and in the market.

Finally, we make sure we act. We develop detailed plans and implement them by having specific responsibilities assigned to people who are held accountable for them.

We deeply believe this time and effort has been worthwhile. SRC has succeeded not because we make some unique product or provide a service no one else has figured out how to do, but rather because we have an extremely innovative and productive culture that allows, indeed requires, people at all levels to think, act, and feel like business owners. Succeeding in this kind of high-involvement culture requires that we have people with very special skills and a strong commitment to the company's success. But by developing this kind of talent, we have created a competitive advantage that has served us remarkably well.

Conclusion

As with succession planning for top management, not every company will be willing or able to go to the lengths described for some of these companies, although they have worked exceptionally well for those involved. But every company needs to identify which of these other processes it should be using to develop and nurture leaders at all levels. For some companies, this will mean bringing in outside consultants, as BL did; for others, the process will be developed internally, as at SRC. However it is done, it needs to be a management priority.

KEY TAKEAWAYS

- *Leadership succession in an ESOP company may be particularly tricky.* New leaders need to honor and develop the ownership culture as well as be able to run the company. Generally, it is better to groom insiders for the job, but this may not always be possible.
- *Make sure the new top leaders have significant time on the job prior to taking on their new duties.* Having a long glide path to leadership helps new leaders prepare for their roles and gives employees more confidence in the transition.
- *Leadership succession at the top levels is critical, but the best companies have plans for leader succession at all levels.* Ideally, each critical person in the company should be identifying potential successors, and employees interested in moving up should have help in developing a career path.

- *Consider developing an inside leadership training program for potential leaders.* Leadership training can be done by your own team members, outside consultants, or both.

Chapter 6

Solutions for the Have/Have-Not Problem

In many mature ESOP companies, once their acquisition loans are paid off, there are only limited ways for new employees to get shares. Most ESOP companies do recycle shares repurchased from former participants, either directly with cash in the ESOP or indirectly by having the company buy back the shares and recontribute them to the ESOP. Shares that employees elect to diversify can also be reallocated broadly. But in most cases, this will only deliver a limited number of shares to newer employees. Often, in order to maintain a steady benefit level, companies will at that point start making cash contributions to the ESOP, meaning the newer employees will have most of their assets in cash.

For some ESOP companies, this is just the way it is, but for companies wanting to maintain a strong, "we're all in this together" ESOP culture, it is very problematic. While the have/have-not problem can be an issue in any ESOP company, it is particularly acute in S corporations with less-than-100% ESOPs. In these companies, distributions are often made to the owners outside the ESOP to pay their taxes. The ESOP has to get a pro-rata share of these distributions. If the ESOP no longer has shares in suspense, then all the distributions must be based on allocated shares. This does not mean that long-term participants get more stock, but they do get the lion's share of the distributions (because, having participated in the ESOP longer, they have more shares in their accounts and thus have more distributions paid to their accounts). When a company uses distributions to repay an ESOP loan, for allocated shares, the participant must receive shares equal in value to the distributions attributable to those shares. For unallocated shares, as long as the allocation formula is nondiscriminatory, the portion of the loan paid with distributions could be allocated on the basis of relative allocations, the company's formula for making contributions to the plan, or another nondiscriminatory formula. Using the release formula used for normal contributions for suspense account shares will result in newer employees getting more shares than if allocations are based solely on allocated shares, but eventually the loan will be repaid, and this opportunity will pass. C corporations also face this same issue about releasing shares from the suspense account when paid with dividends, but dividends are typically a smaller part of the total repayment strategy in C corporations, so the have/have-not problem that results is not as serious.

This chapter looks at several ways to deal with this problem. First, it covers what I call share strategies—ways to deliver more shares to employees through additional contributions, releveraging, forfeiture rules, and early diversification. Second, it looks at rebalancing and account segregation.

Share Strategies

Buy More Shares

If companies are less than 100% owned by the ESOP, they can always do another share acquisition. In some companies, the seller(s) like the idea of the company becoming a 100% ESOP-owned S corporation, but they still want an equity stake. One approach is to have them finance the acquisition with a seller note and get part of their return in warrants. Warrants give them the right to the increase in the value of a certain number of shares over a stated period of time.

Contribute More Shares

Companies can also contribute additional shares to the ESOP. This is tax-deductible, but will dilute the ownership stake of other owners. The ESOP will get a bigger share of subsequent distributions as well. The allocation of additional shares can be set up in the plan document so that it is skewed downward. You can, for instance, put a cap on how much pay qualifies for the contribution (so if you contribute 10% of pay, and the cap is $50,000 and I make $75,000, I still only get $5,000). You can also give extra credit for fewer years of service. This approach needs to be tested to make sure it does not somehow favor more highly-paid people, which is very unlikely.

Some 100% ESOP-owned companies have used this strategy, although there are no tax benefits if they are S corporations because there are no taxes in that case. Contributing new shares means newer employees will get more shares, but more senior people will be diluted.

Releverage

There is a lot of discussion these days of releveraging—taking out a new ESOP loan to buy out some or all existing shares in the ESOP and (in one variant of releveraging) starting a new ESOP with what has been purchased. (See the discussion at the end of chapter 3.) So far, few companies have done this, but it is an intriguing strategy for companies with the right cash flow. In addition to getting shares to new people at a now much lower price, it gives existing employees an immediate payout at the current price. If a company's stock price is going up faster than its cost of money, then buying back shares may be a good strategy—and it is common in public companies. Releveraging can be for all or part of the shares.

Early Diversification

On a voluntary basis, companies can offer early diversification at any age. Then these shares can be allocated to other employees much as you do with forfeitures. This works well for companies whose stock price growth is strong and cash flow or cash reserves are able to handle the repurchase obligation comfortably. Some companies do this, in fact, as a way to manage long-term repurchase costs.

Forfeiture Formulas

Formulas for allocating forfeited shares can be set up to favor newer and/or lower-paid employees, provided the plan administrator tests this for compliance with ESOP allocation rules. Normally, that would not be a problem.

Rebalancing, Segregation (Reshuffling), and Profit Sharing Accounting

Rebalancing

Rebalancing is an increasingly common approach in ESOP companies. Assume that MatureCo's ESOP has paid off all of its loans and now owns 100% of the company's shares. Cash may be going into the plan for a few different reasons:

- If MatureCo had been an S corporation and did a gradual ESOP, the ESOP probably has substantial cash from distributions. For instance, imagine that MatureCo's ESOP bought 30% in the first go-round. The company made $2 million in the next year. The 70% non-ESOP owner got a K-1 statement saying that she owed taxes on $1.4 million (70% of $2 million). The ESOP owns 30%, but it pays no taxes on the $600,000 in profits attributable to the plan. The owner requests a distribution of $640,000 (40% of $1.4 million) to pay her taxes. Under S corporation law, the ESOP must get a pro-rata distribution of $240,000. Over time, this can add a lot of cash to the plan.
- Some ESOP companies maintain target rates of annual contributions to their ESOP. If a company had been putting in, say, 10% of pay per year to pay off a loan, it might want to continue to contribute 8% of pay on an ongoing basis. Some of that cash might be used to buy shares from participants getting distributions, but there may be cash left over.
- Less commonly, some C corporations, and a few S corporations, will contribute dividends or earnings distributions into the ESOP.

To rebalance, at the end of the plan year, shares are sold within the plan for cash so that, within some limits, everyone has the same percentage of stock and cash. For instance, say John has $10,000, all in cash, and Mary has $100,000, all in stock. Overall, 80% of plan assets are in company stock. The ESOP trustee would buy and sell shares within the trust so that John would now have $2,000 in cash and $8,000 in stock and Mary $80,000 in stock and $20,000 in cash.

Account Segregation (Reshuffling)

Account segregation (called "reshuffling" of terminated participant accounts in IRS guidance[1]) applies only to shares held by former plan

---

1. The IRS has defined reshuffling as "the mandatory transfer of employer securities into or out of plan accounts, not designed to result in an equal proportion

participants who are still in the plan. In account segregation, the ESOP cashes in these shares and reallocates them to people in the plan who are still working for the company. The former employees now have cash in the plan that must be invested prudently. Some ESOPs just put this money in a CD, but Department of Labor officials have indicated informally that this is not a prudent approach. Ideally, plan trustees should use an investment advisor to recommend an approach that is conservative but diversified into a higher-yielding mix of investments.

It may seem that if the company has the money to cash out the shares, it should just do that rather than retain and manage the cash until a later (often five years later) payout. Companies do this primarily to discourage employees from leaving just to get access to their accounts.

Profit Sharing Accounting

Another common approach is "profit sharing" accounting, in which each employee ends up with the same percentage of shares and other investments as each other employee. In profit sharing accounting, individual employee accounts do not get regular allocations of stock and/or cash. Instead, employees have a percentage of the total assets of the trust, with each participant holding the same percentage of cash and shares. So if the plan has $5 million in assets, of which 20% is in cash, each employee-participant has a share equal to 20% cash and 80% stock. It is preferable to use profit sharing accounting from the beginning of the plan rather than switch to it later, which would involve complex reallocations and compliance with the rules governing them.

IRS Guidelines on Rebalancing and Reshuffling

In 2010, the IRS made it clear that rebalancing and reshuffling are allowable, provided certain rules are met.[2] The IRS made several key points to keep in mind:

---

of employer securities in each account." Account segregation as explained here is reshuffling that applies only to terminated employees.

2. The IRS provided this guidance in one of a series of internal memoranda written in response to requests for technical assistance within the agency; the memoranda were widely disseminated among ESOP practitioners.

- Plan provisions that provide for the mandatory transfer of stock must be in a "written program" with a "definite predetermined allocation formula." Any provision providing for the mandatory transfer of stock must include the number of shares (presumably a formula to be applied in each year) or amount of cash to transfer in or out of plan accounts. The provision must also state the manner in which the transfer will be effectuated (such as the date of valuation).
- The right of each participant to have a particular form of investment does not raise the issue of "effective availability of benefits" so long as all participants are treated in the same way. For segregation, because these participants are a separate class of employee, nondiscriminatory reshuffling also does not affect current availability.
- The right to retain employer stock is not a protected benefit. However, the rebalancing cannot be done in such a way that someone who has diversified his or her account into cash now will have some of that cash moved back into stock.

It is far better to put rebalancing language in a plan document before you plan to do it. There are still some advisors who believe that taking away the right to shares after they have been allocated is protected. If the plan provides for this in advance, there should be no issue. Nonetheless, many plans do put the language into their plan the year they start to rebalance.

Employee communications are also critical, especially if your stock value has outperformed the kinds of investments the cash is invested in. Long-term participants may feel they are losing out. It is critical to help people understand why becoming more diversified is prudent and that sustainability of the employee ownership culture that has served them so well needs to avoid a "have/have-not" allocation of shares.

Caveats

Neither rebalancing nor segregation can be used on a targeted basis to move shares out of the accounts of selected participants in order to reduce their ownership to help meet the S corporation anti-abuse rules under Section 409(p) of the Code. The policies must apply to everyone.

The cash in the ESOP should also be prudently invested. Many companies just move it into CDs. That is a doubtful strategy, as noted above. No prudent fiduciary would invest all retirement assets in CDs. Companies can and should leave money in readily liquid and safe investments for anticipated short-term needs, but should consult an investment advisor to develop a strategy for the conservative and prudent diversification of the remaining cash.

KEY TAKEAWAYS

- There are several solutions to the have/have-not problem, including rebalancing, contributing new shares, early diversification, post-termination reshuffling (account segregation), and profit sharing accounting. The earlier you plan on these as options, the less resistance you will encounter when the changes are made.
- Consider releveraging your plan to buy back shares if you are a mature ESOP with adequate cash flow.
- Buy stock back at the corporate level if you are a 100% ESOP-owned S corporation (and often even in other scenarios); then recontribute it as needed on a more level basis than would result from having the ESOP buy back whatever shares are available each year.

Chapter 7

Sustainable ESOP Governance

ESOP companies can be and often are governed in much the same way they were before adopting an ESOP. In that case, a board composed of insiders has formal control of the company, although practical control may rest with the CEO. ESOP fiduciaries may be officers of the company appointed by the board.

In recent years, there has been a striking trend in ESOP companies toward adding outside, independent board members and a less dramatic, but growing, trend to have independent ESOP trustees or at least outside directed trustees. There are a number of reasons for this change:

- At the board level, more and more companies have decided that outside board members can add perspective, expertise, and credibility for a very modest cost. Many business owners feared that having a more independent board would mean the company would go in a direction they did not want, but experience shows that is rarely the case, although boards may persuade existing management that making one change or another makes sense.
- As the ESOP completes buying out the seller(s), having more professional governance brought in is usually less threatening to the prior or soon-to-be prior owners. In part, this is because at that point sellers are less concerned about retaining some level of control to help assure the debt is paid off and they are not left on the hook, either because they have a note or have collateralized a bank loan. Another reason is that because sellers may now be ready to move on to other things in life, even if they retain some lesser involvement with the business.
- Although litigation involving ESOPs is still relatively rare (fewer than 25 cases per year reach court, out of about 7,000 ESOPs),

Department of Labor (DOL) audits are more common because the DOL has made clear it will examine ESOPs more closely than other plans. Having outside trustees provides some protection against adverse outcomes.

- Many inside ESOP fiduciaries, often CFOs or other officers, simply don't want to take the time and make the commitment to learn all they need to learn and do all the work they need to do to be good fiduciaries. ESOP companies consistently report that even though independent trustees only rarely impose changes a company's management opposes, having outside trustees seems less worrisome to insiders.
- Outside trustees bring a higher level of expertise to the fiduciary process and can be very helpful in assuring proper plan operations and valuations.

The trends in corporate governance can be seen by comparing the NCEO's first survey on this issue in 2003 and our most recent in 2012. In 2003, 51% of companies had at least one independent board member; in 2012, 62% did. More dramatically, only 17% of companies in 2003 had an institutional trustee; in 2012, 37% did. Of that 37%, about half were directed trustees and half were independent (we did not ask about directed versus non-directed in 2003).

Creating an Effective Board of Directors

There are four key issues to consider in creating and sustaining an effective board:

- What is the role of the board?
- How should the board be structured?
- Who should be on the board?
- How should the board be compensated?

Role and Structure of the Board

In non-ESOP companies, boards are generally passive formalities. But when an ESOP company decides to move toward a more active ESOP board, there are a few different roles the board can play. All boards, however, have certain key duties under state laws. These include:

- *The duty of care.* The duty of care requires that boards exercise their duties in a way that avoids harm to shareholders. That is a broad definition, of course, but some key elements include understanding the company's financials and operations, reviewing executive compensation, hiring and firing the CEO and possibly other officers, making sure the audit procedures are proper, and reviewing the overall business plan of the company.
- *The duty of loyalty.* Boards must be loyal to shareholder interests first. This is primarily defined in terms of maximizing the long-term value of shareholder assets, but many states allow other corporate goals at least to be considered. In some states, there are "B" (for benefit) corporation statutes that allow companies to incorporate in a way that explicitly places other concerns, typically focused around social responsibility issues, into the board's deliberations. Note that while these state laws may protect boards that do not automatically accept outside offers for the company at significant premiums, ESOP trustees are subject to more narrow rules.

The most common conflicts concerning the duty of loyalty arise from boards approving excessive compensation or benefits for executives, but could also include any corporate action designed to benefit individual interests other than shareholders, such as favoring a supplier owned by a colleague of an executive or leasing assets from a non-ESOP owner at excessive cost.

Beyond these basics, there are several possible levels of board involvement. Jack Veale, an ESOP consultant who has specialized in ESOP company boards, notes several typical structures for boards, ESOPs or not:[1]

- *The certifying board:* This board has independent directors whose job typically is to serve as a reality check for the decisions the CEO and other top managers make. For the most part, they rely on man-

---

1. The categories are Jack Veale's; the specific language is ours at the NCEO.

agement but act as a check on decisions that could be damaging. For instance, they may decide an executive pay proposal is excessive, an acquisition is ill-advised, or a strategic change is impractical. In that case, they would become more engaged to try to move toward a better path. Boards like this can be very valuable in well-managed companies that really do not need a lot of outside input but can benefit from a reality check from time to time, an occasional new perspective or idea, and the credibility that having outside board members can provide to lenders, employees, and other constituencies. Not every company, in other words, may benefit from a more engaged board.

- *The engaged board:* This board may have more outsiders, which may even comprise a majority of its members. Increasingly, this is the norm in ESOP company boards. These boards see their role as having an active role in making suggestions, dividing into committees that seriously consider such issues as strategy, compensation, culture, and strategy. There is a high level of interaction and discussion at board meetings. The engaged board takes time to define the roles and responsibilities of board members and the boundaries and responsibilities of both the board and the CEO. An engaged board is likely to have several committees, such as audit, compensation committee, and governance. This board understands it is ultimately responsible for oversight of the CEO and company performance as well as succession planning. This board will sometimes seek outside experts who can add value to its decision-making process.

    Some examples of what this board might do include:

    — Engaging a compensation consultant to help evaluate proposals for executive compensation and developing guidelines for pay as to both amount and structure (incentive pay, equity awards, base pay, etc.)

    — Reviewing strategic planning processes and noting gaps and opportunities

    — Overseeing the audit process

    — Helping the company develop and maintain a successful ownership culture

- Reviewing the performance of top executives and oversee succession
- Evaluating ESOP-specific issues, such as handling the repurchase obligation
- Developing committees to work with managers on specific business issues
- Responding to acquisition offers
- Evaluating potential acquisitions of other companies

- *The operating board:* Operating boards often have a majority of outside directors who are actively engaged in the operational decisions of the company. They take on all the duties outlined for engaged boards but differ in that they see their role as actually making decisions rather than providing input. Generally, these boards have a number of subject matter experts with experience in the industry. Operating boards are not common and can be a two-edged sword. With the right people, they can be particularly useful in strategic planning, marketing, compensation policy, and product development. On the other hand, if a board actively seeks to intervene in multiple decisions normally made by management, that can create intense conflicts and a lot of wheel-spinning, and it can lead to decisions that reflect more the egos of board members than the best ideas.

- *The intervening or crisis board:* These boards are often brought in when there are difficult situations that cannot be handled by the existing board, often due to internal conflicts between board members or conflicts between owners. For instance, outsiders might be brought in to help navigate disputes between two or more non-ESOP owners, to help make a more informed decision about putting the company up for sale, to help deal with a management crisis, or other difficult situations.

There is no right decision about what the board should do, but there are wrong ones. Board functions and personalities need to mesh well with management and fill in the gaps that management might have. All boards, however, should ideally provide an independent review of top-level compensation and make sure auditing procedures are proper.

Whatever role is chosen for the board, it is essential to make sure the skills and inclinations of board members are consistent with what they are expected to do. If board members are going to be involved in business decisions, they need either to come with the relevant expertise or be trained to develop it. Boards also should provide training to all board members to understand company specifics. All boards, no matter what their role, need to understand how ESOPs work and should, at the least, have some training in that (the NCEO has a book and a training program for board members, or you can engage your counsel).

Inclinations matter as well, however. A board that wants to be highly engaged when it lacks the skills and/or experience creates continued conflicts with management and is not going to be a productive asset for the company. A company that needs more engaged boards and hires people looking for "something (but not too much) to do" in retirement will be equally frustrated.

Composition and Selection of the Board

A first decision is whether the board should have a majority of outsiders. However, this may be a less important issue than it seems. It is rare for ESOP boards to make decisions other than by consensus. I serve on three boards, for instance, and we have never done otherwise (two have a majority of insiders). Having a majority of outside members may be useful, however, regarding potentially contentious issues, particularly surrounding issues where insiders have strong conflicts of interest, such as executive pay. Having a committee of outsiders first make recommendations on these issues may help resolve that problem.

A second key issue is who should serve on the board. Almost all ESOP companies have the CEO on the board, and it is hard to imagine how a board could function without this. Other common inside board members include the CFO and director of HR. As noted, a small percentage of companies have nonmanagement employees on the board.

In looking for outside directors, several different kinds of skills might be sought:

- *Business subject matter experts:* These people typically have worked in the industry and, in some cases, for the company.

- *ESOP experts:* Having someone who is very familiar with ESOPs can help companies learn what the best practices in the field are. This might be an ESOP professional (but not your advisors) or an ESOP company executive (the NCEO maintains a directory of retired ESOP executives).
- *Financial experts:* Some companies want an accountant on the board (but not theirs) to help review audits and financial statements.
- *Rainmakers:* These are people with connections that can be useful in securing new business.
- *Thought leaders:* These might be academics, organizational development consultants, or other people who can bring new ideas to the board and, often, help facilitate discussions.

In addition, boards should have at least one person willing to challenge the conventional wisdom and one person good at facilitating consensus.

Getting Employees Involved on the Board

NCEO data indicate that only a few percent of ESOP companies have nonmanagement employees on the board, while 16% of ESOP companies allow employees to vote for the board. Having nonmanagement employees on a board can make the plan seem more legitimate to employees and can provide valuable feedback to other board members. The fiduciary duties of board members are substantial, however, and boards should not bring people on who lack the necessary skills, such as understanding financial statements, and are unable to obtain them. Employees need to understand as well that no matter how good the board's insurance policy is, there are risks that come with being a board member.

Having employees vote for the board can be a good way to increase credibility. Proponents of employee voting often argue that unless employees can elect the board, their ownership is not "real," while opponents worry that if they do elect the board, insurgencies can lead to new board members who will take the company in undesired directions.

It turns out that having employees vote for the board matters less than expected in terms of the kinds of decisions that get made. Generally, boards nominate a slate of directors and employees vote for them. Insurgent candidates are very rare, and even if they do get elected, rarely lead to significant changes. The decision on voting, therefore, may be more symbolic than practical.

An alternative to having employees on the board is to select employees to attend board meetings, either on a regular basis or selectively. The employees could be elected by other employees, appointed by the ESOP committee, or selected by management. They can be excluded from sensitive issues such as pay discussions.

This approach allows the board to hear the views of employees in a more direct way than just listening to management talk about what employees think. Employees may provide valuable insights and ideas into how the company is working, as well as taking back their experiences with what a board really does to their colleagues.

Aside from having employees at the board meeting, boards can, and I think should, have regular opportunities to meet employees. This can be at annual meetings, at lunches during board meetings, tours of facilities, etc. Hearing from employees should be an essential duty of any good ESOP company board.

Board Compensation

Compensation matters can be a thorny issue, especially in private companies. While board member compensation is a matter of public record in public companies, private companies have no obligation to disclose this information and often decline to do so. Two general rules seem to apply: the larger the company the higher the compensation, and the higher the risk (as in public companies) the higher the compensation. A good starting point is the data from the annual National Association of Corporate Directors compensation surveys for public companies, and, more usefully, its biannual survey of compensation and governance activity in private companies. The compensation in public companies should probably be viewed as an upper boundary by private companies since some level of discount factor applies due to the increased risk of serving on a public company board. The NCEO also has data on board compensation for ESOP companies. Typical compensation is either a set retainer or fees per meeting (or a combination). For ESOPs in the

20–500 employee range, annual compensation typically ranges from about $6,000 per year to $15,000 per year. In larger companies, fees may be twice that. The median compensation is $12,000.

Trustee and Fiduciary Issues

ESOP companies have two layers of governance: the board and plan fiduciaries, which includes both the plan's trustee(s) and any individual or group causing the trustees to make a decision. Companies need to choose whether to have institutional trustees (which can be independent or directed) or appoint insiders to that duty. First, though, it is critical to understand who is a fiduciary.

ERISA defines a fiduciary as anyone who makes a decision or causes a decision to be made concerning plan assets. Clearly, then, if someone directs a trustee as to how to make a decision, the person providing the direction is a fiduciary. But the concept of causing a decision to be made is more complex. For instance, if a board or CEO withholds crucial financial information from a trustee that leads to a decision being made that should not have been made, the board or CEO can share fiduciary responsibility. If an inside trustee is pressured to make a decision by a superior, that superior could be a fiduciary. In a number of public company cases, boards were co-fiduciaries because either they or the executives they were supposed to be controlling were encouraging employees to invest in shares that they had reason to believe were not good investments and/or were allowing accounting procedures that provided flawed pictures of the state of the company.

Similarly, courts have ruled that boards have a fiduciary duty to select and monitor trustees to make sure that they are qualified, are acting in the best interests of plan participants, and have procedures in place to make prudent decisions. That does not mean the board shares fiduciary duties on a decision-by-decision basis, but it does mean the board needs to be able to make a good argument that it appointed the right trustee and made sure they were doing the kinds of things the law and plan require.

Fiduciary Duties

There are a number of fiduciary decisions. First, we can exclude things that are not fiduciary duties. These include preparing reports for the government and employees; overseeing allocations, vesting, benefit distributions, and other "ministerial" functions; calculating and explaining benefits; processing claims; and other record-keeping tasks.

For decisions that are subject to fiduciary purview, fiduciaries must act according to the "prudent person" standard, i.e., "with the care, skill, prudence, and diligence under the circumstances then prevailing that a prudent man acting in a like capacity and familiar with such matters would use in the conduct of an enterprise of like character and with like aims." Fiduciaries must act for the "exclusive benefit of plan participants," meaning when there is a conflict between participant and other interests, participant interests, as defined by their investment interest in the plan, must be favored.

There are a number of specific fiduciary duties, including:

1. Buying and selling plan assets, including employer stock
2. Hiring qualified advisers
3. Determining that the ESOP is paying no more than fair market value
4. Assuring that the plan is operated in accordance with plan documents and ERISA; if the two conflict, ERISA rules govern
5. Making sure the terms of any ESOP loan are reasonable
6. Voting and/or directing the tendering of shares in the trust for which plan and ERISA rules do not require pass-through voting
7. Deciding whether to follow participant voting or tendering directions on unallocated or undirected shares
8. Responding to legitimate offers to purchase the company
9. Acting to protect plan interests with respect to corporate actions that could harm the interests of plan participants

Number 4 of these duties (assuring that the plan is operated in accordance with plan documents and ERISA), of course, is very broad. It can include a variety of decisions. For instance, a fiduciary could be sued for failing to allow employees to vote their shares on required issues, for not giving employees appropriate information to make a decision when they vote, for failing to distribute benefits according to plan rules, for acting in a discriminatory manner in honoring the put option, for failing to assure the filing of reports so that the plan loses its qualified status, and so on.

Number 9 is also a potentially confusing issue. As noted above, ESOP trustees generally refrain from taking an active role in business decisions. The business judgment rule makes it difficult for trustees to challenge the board on business decisions. There are instances, however, when boards take actions that trustees believe constitute a waste of corporate assets egregious enough to push for reconsideration. These include such matters as excessive executive compensation, business practices aimed at benefitting certain individuals in the company at the expense of shareholders (such as excessive perquisites or contracts with businesses owned by the seller or the seller's family that are not economically competitive), major strategic decisions that are poorly conceived, etc. A good trustee will monitor board activities sufficiently to raise red flags before the decisions are made so that a solution can be worked out beforehand.

Who Should Be the ESOP Trustee?

The 2012 NCEO ESOP Corporate Governance Survey looked at who serves as an ESOP trustee. Table 7-1 shows the results.

Table 7-1. Who serves as the ESOP trustee			
	$50 million sales or less	Over $200 million sales	Overall sample
Institutional trustee	25%	64%	37%
Non-employee individual	6%	7%	7%
Individual employee	30%	4%	21%
Employee-only committee	33%	15%	29%
Committee of employees and non-employees	5%	8%	6%

Inside employee fiduciary committees are management-only 75% of the time. Non-employee trustees are often former sellers, board members, or executives.

Fifty-six percent of the companies direct the trustee as to decisions for the ESOP (this includes both outside trustees and inside trustees).

In 48% of the companies where there is a directed trustee, the board provides the directions, while in 39% of the companies it is an ESOP committee. The remaining 13% are directed by management or other unspecified individual.

Independent Trustees

ESOP companies are increasingly using outside professional trustees. There are a number of reasons for this, but the most important are concerns about fiduciary liability for inside trustees and the belief that it is better to pay for the expertise that a qualified trustee can bring to the ESOP process than, in effect, pay internal staff to develop the skills and do all the things a trustee must do. While independent trustees are an added cost of potentially tens of thousands of dollars annually (fees depend on the size of the company, scope of engagement, and perceived risk of the engagement, among other things), that may be less than the implied cost of the staff time needed to perform these functions. The NCEO governance survey found the median trustee compensation for smaller companies (up to $50 million in sales) was about $15,000 per year, rising incrementally with size to $35,000 for sales between $50 million and $200 million, and $80,000 for companies larger than that. Fees did not vary significantly based on whether the trustee was independent or directed.

Independent trustees can be a bank or other professional trust institution or, occasionally, an individual specialized in this field. Trustees should be able to show substantial experience in the field, be willing to share (and explain if necessary) any audit or court cases they have been involved in, and be active in the relevant professional organizations. Boards need to select trustees whose style and approach is comfortable to them. If a trustee wants a more active role on the board than the company wants, for instance, or has views on issues such as the repurchase obligation, valuation approaches and assumptions, executive pay, and other issues on which the board feels differently and has good reason to believe its views are consistent with ERISA, then a different trustee should be chosen.

Directed Trustees

A directed trustee is chosen from the same pool as independent trustees and does all of what an independent trustee does, but is told what to do by a board, an ESOP plan administrative committee, or an individual employee. The directing party retains fiduciary responsibility. Directed trustees still must make sure plan rules and ERISA are followed. Directed trustees add expertise and save costs for inside fiduciaries, but do not reduce fiduciary risk. Although they are directed, they are not exempt from fiduciary risk. While they owe deference to the decisions made by whoever is directing them, if they believe the directions are clearly outside of what the plan or ERISA requires, they have to act in the same way an independent trustee would.

In some companies, the trustees are employees, but are directed as to what to do by an ESOP administrative committee. This may be because the company wants one person to handle the formal, ministerial duties of being a trustee but others to act as decision-makers. Both parties, however, are fiduciaries.

Inside Trustees

Some companies appoint a single person to be the trustee, often the CFO. Other companies have a committee, usually of two to four people acting as the trustees. Usually, the committee members are officers, but some companies allow employees to select one or more of their colleagues to serve on the trust committee.

Employees need to understand the weighty responsibilities they are taking on and the potential personal liabilities. They need to commit to substantial training (see the section below on inside trustee training) and be willing to spend many, many hours reviewing the appraisal report, working with the plan administrator, reviewing executive compensation, electing the board, and possibly playing a role in corporate decisions, such as acquisitions of or by the company.

The Role of Sellers

Trustees can be anyone or any institution. In the past, it was not uncommon for sellers to also act as trustees. That is not a wise choice. Sellers have a direct conflict of interest on many ESOP matters, especially the price for the shares and, when there are seller notes, the terms of the loan. The ESOP trustee wants the best deal possible for the participants; sellers would be presumed to want a good deal for themselves. Courts look to process far more than outcomes, so even if the seller has the purest of intentions, the appearance of a conflict of interest will make prevailing in a lawsuit unlikely.

In some cases, however, sellers may act as fiduciaries for decisions that do not involve transactions between them and the ESOP. For instance, a company may set up a trustee committee of insiders, but the seller will not be a trustee for any issues concerning his or her shares or shares of family members. Even here, however, conflicts of interest can be problematic. If the seller still has a direct interest, then many critical decisions, such as selecting an appraiser, reviewing and deciding on the appraiser's report, responding to offers to buy the company, and executive pay (if the seller still is an employee) can all create potential conflict. If the seller has sold all the shares and is no longer an employee, the conflicts are usually less significant, but best practice would suggest that the seller should not be a trustee, nor be on an ESOP committee directing the trustee.

The fear that sellers have, of course, is losing control of critical decisions. If sellers have a note outstanding, it is understandable why they would have this concern. One way to deal with this is for the seller, board, and trustee to agree on certain loan covenants that prohibit the board from taking specific actions, such as paying dividends, taking on new debt, or making major acquisitions without seller approval. In practice, though, NCEO has found that it is very rare for sellers to find that trustees cause the company to head in directions that the seller would not otherwise accept. Trustees do not want to be involved in second-guessing board decisions, and, even if they wanted to, the business judgment rule makes it difficult to prevail. Trustees will almost always get involved only if they perceive egregious issues. Boards nominate their successors. The seller almost always will have determined who the board is before the ESOP transaction. Even if boards then expand to add outsiders, the decisions are being made by people the seller trusted. Finally, the seller can and often does retain a seat on the board. Given the risks of sellers acting as ESOP fiduciaries compared to the potential benefits (at least for the seller), the NCEO strongly recommends that sellers not take on this role.

Who Should Direct the Trustee

As noted above, about half of all trustees who are directed are directed by the board, another 39% by an ESOP committee, and the rest by management or other unspecified individuals. There is no obvious best choice on this, but if boards direct the trustee, there are potential conflict-of-interest situations. For instance, a board may want to protect certain interests or values in the face of an acquisition offer, but the trustee may take a different view. Boards often have top executives on them who would be conflicted in making recommendations on executive pay. Of course, ESOP committees may face the same kinds of conflicts because of the personal situations of their members. But because boards and trustees have fiduciary duties that are not always identical, the NCEO recommends that boards not direct trustees. The NCEO also does not recommend an executive take on that role.

Rather than board members or executives, an ESOP committee makes the most sense (these are often referred to as an ESOP administrative committees in plan documents to distinguish them from ESOP communications committees). These committees would normally consist of a small group of managers, although as noted above, some companies have nonmanagement employees on the committees as well (see the discussion below on whether nonmanagement employees should have a fiduciary role).

Inside Trustee Training

Companies that have inside trustees need to make sure they are properly trained. At a minimum, they need a clear understanding of:

- The plan document and what it requires
- What ERISA requires for ESOPs
- How to read and understand a valuation report
- How ESOP valuations differ from normal valuations
- How repurchase obligation works and how the company can manage it
- Best practices for boards of directors
- Best practices for executive compensation

Realistically, this means employees should commit to spending what will normally amount to several days a year of time on keeping up to date on key issues, reviewing the appraisal report, selecting directors, making sure executive pay is reasonable, and interacting with the plan administrator to make sure proper procedures are followed.

Fortunately, there are now many ways for inside fiduciaries to obtain this training, including webinars, seminars and conferences, books, and formal training programs. The NCEO, for instance, has an extensive set of resources available on this.

Trustees on Boards

There is no consensus on whether trustees should be on boards. Institutional trustees do not want to serve on boards, as they believe it creates a potential conflict of interest given the differing fiduciary duties of the two bodies. Companies with inside trustees, however, often have one or more trustees on the board because their position in the company, such as CFO, makes them valuable to both groups. In some ESOP litigation, the issue of people wearing multiple hats has made it more difficult for ESOP defendants to prevail.

A compromise approach would be to have the trustee sit in on board meetings either all the time (in the case of insiders) or for part of a periodic board meeting (for outsiders), but not formally be on the board. In the latter case, this is a good opportunity for the board and trustee to exchange concerns and discuss overlapping issues.

Should Nonmanagement Employees Be Fiduciaries?

Some companies have non-management employees serve on a trust committee or on a plan committee that directs a formal trustee. Doing this can provide additional credibility to the plan as well as getting a perspective that would often not be present in conventional governance arrangements. There are risks as well, however. First, the employees do take on potential legal liability. While insurance and/or indemnification may protect them, there is always a very remote chance that they can end up with personal exposure if these policy limits are exceeded (there have been a few instances of this). Employees need to have this risk laid out very clearly, even if it is very small.

A more immediate issue is that being a fiduciary is a major responsibility that will take considerable time both at meetings and in learning the rules. No one should serve in any fiduciary capacity unless they can commit what is probably a couple of weeks' time over a year to these duties. Employees who are selected must also be comfortable that they have the skills and interest to learn the relevant material.

Responding to Offers

The most difficult issue boards can face is an acquisition offer. Responding is more difficult in an ESOP company because while both the board and the ESOP trustee have fiduciary responsibilities concerning how to respond, the rules for what each should do are not exactly the same. The ESOP fiduciary must respond as to the shares the trust owns, with the response being based on maximizing the long-term value of the plan assets. Employment, social value, or other issues cannot be considered. That does not mean the fiduciary must say yes to any offer higher than fair market value. The fiduciary needs to weigh how employees would do over the next three to five years or so based on whether they would end up better off staying in the ESOP or selling. The basic model asks what employee account balances would look like in the ESOP over that period of time versus what they would be if the company was sold and the assets reinvested in a secure (and thus low return) investment over that period. This calculation looks at:

- How quickly is ESOP share value expected to grow?
- What are the expected contributions to the ESOP over the next few years as a percentage of pay? If that is higher than normal retirement plan contributions, this extra value needs to be factored in. This is especially true in a leveraged ESOP where the contributions are required at some level.
- If the offer is clearly better, *and* it does not include contingencies that could make the offer less attractive than it seems, then the trustee probably should say yes.

The board, on the other hand, can take a broader view, at least in most states, albeit asset maximization must still be the primary concern. In practice, the way this usually works out is that the CEO receives offers and decides which, if any, are serious. These should be limited to offers made specifically for the company, that are above fair market value, that are not brokerage requests looking for companies to buy, that do not have contingencies that make them much less certain and attractive than they might seem, and that come from buyers who appear well financed. The board then looks at these serious offers and decides whether they are attractive enough to send on to the trustee.

For serious offers, once the consideration has begun, the board should review what representations and warranties the company is making to any lenders and what level of indemnification the company is giving to the ESOP buyer and the lenders. This will consist of a laundry list of items, including that the company has paid its taxes on a timely basis, that the company's financial statements are accurate, that the company is not under investigation for any wrongdoing, and that the company is not in violation of any environmental laws.

The company should have a written policy outlining how it responds to offers. The policy should state that the company is not for sale (unless it is) but that serious offers will be considered. Potential buyers should be asked to indicate why they want to buy your specific company, how the deal will be financed, and whether there will be any contingencies. The policy should outline the steps the board will take to respond to an offer, which may include having a committee vet the proposal first and hiring an outside advisor to help evaluate the proposal.

If the company is majority employee-owned, the policy should also be clear that the company is a majority or 100% ESOP-owned company and that the ESOP fiduciary will make the ultimate decision as to the disposition of any shares it owns. The procedures for that should be outlined in a way that makes it clear this will be a complicated and lengthy process with multiple advisors involved. If the fiduciary is an insider, the NCEO strongly recommends that an independent transactional trustee be appointed. If the company is less than majority-owned by the ESOP, all the other steps previously outlined in this section still have to be taken, but the ESOP trustee will not be able to control the outcome unless there is a division between non-ESOP owners and the ESOP trustee provides the decisive directions.

Many majority-ESOP companies also have a written statement saying they are an employee-owned company and prefer to stay that way.

The NCEO's *ESOP Company Board Handbook* has sample language for this.[2]

The approach the board will follow, regardless of how much the ESOP owns, will also depend on the company's posture relative to a sale. Key scenarios are described below:

- *Not for sale:* If the company does not want to be sold, it needs to make that clear to potential acquirers—but also be clear that it has a legal responsibility to consider strong offers. If one or more is received, the board needs to carefully examine the terms of the offer. It can also consider the plans the acquirer has for the company and whether those fit its corporate culture or other objectives. If it does not, or the board continues not to want to be sold, it needs to assess whether the financial value of the offer is so strong that it would be unreasonable to say no. It would be advisable at this point to engage the trustee.

    If the offer is so strong that it requires serious consideration, the board needs to be sure the acquirer knows the process the company will go through. The board may decide it wants to solicit other bids or possibly ask for an employee advisory vote if a vote is not already legally required. All of this is likely to deter all but the very strongest offers. It is rare for an ESOP company to be acquired that does not want to be acquired.

- *Open to good deals:* Much the same process would be followed if the board is open to strong proposals, but now the board would encourage the buyers more and possibly seek other buyers.

- *Wanting to find a buyer:* Here the board's role is very different. For whatever reason, a company may decide it is time to sell. In many cases, the CEO will be charged with initiating the search for buyers; in others, an investment banking firm will be engaged. The board will be more open to deals that offer a premium, but not necessarily one substantially above current fair market value.

---

2. Corey Rosen et al., *The ESOP Company Board Handbook* (NCEO, 2014) (see nceo.org/r/sourcebook).

Conclusion

Governance has become a much more prominent issue for ESOP companies wanting to stay ESOP-owned for the long term. Having outside board members is widely seen as best practice, and more companies are moving toward having outside trustees as well. Whatever decision a company ultimately makes, it is essential that key players understand that ESOP companies are different, legally and often culturally. They need to take the time to understand the law, the plan, and how the decisions they make may differ because they are an ESOP company.

While this may seem burdensome, companies that have moved in this direction almost always report that the changes have strengthened not just the ESOP but also the entire company by adding valuable expertise and perspective.

KEY TAKEAWAYS

- *Adding outside board members can provide a valuable source of input and credibility.* Board members generally cost less than hiring people with similar expertise as consultants.
- *Decide how active you want your board to be.* Should it be primarily a sounding board or should it play a more active role in strategy, compensation, culture, and/or other issues?
- *Makes sure board members have the training to know what their ESOP duties are.* The NCEO has a board training package and can do a customized board training program through an online presentation.
- *Outside trustees can provide valuable expertise and save time for insiders who would otherwise perform these duties.* That benefit needs to be weighed against costs and whether the board and management are willing to have this additional input and, in some cases, decision- making authority.
- *If you use inside trustees, training is essential.* Being a trustee is a significant responsibility, and trustees should be ready to spend considerable time on the job, particularly in reviewing valuation.

- *Understand that just because there is a formal trustee does not mean that other people will not act as fiduciaries or be deemed to be fiduciaries.* Fiduciaries are not just those making a decision but also are those causing a decision to be made.
- *Establish a written policy for how boards will respond to acquisition offers.*
- *Always use independent transactional trustees when responding to a serious outside offer.*

Chapter 8

Communicating ESOPs

In 2015, a company called Sentry Services lost a lawsuit over allegations it never told the participants it has an ESOP (nor paid them out). That's the only time we at the NCEO have ever encountered an ESOP that did *that* poor a job of communicating, but when we ask ESOP companies how they think their communications programs are working, few are completely satisfied. That's understandable. Just about every company has a wide mix of employees. There are usually mixes of education, income, social backgrounds, and many other differences. Aside from these demographic variations, there are almost always wide variations in levels of interest in learning about ESOPs as well as styles of learning (visual, experiential, auditory, reading, and so on). There are also a lot of preconceived notions about ESOPs that have to be overcome, as well as rumors and misunderstandings that pass between people and get accepted as what ESOPs really are.

The good news is that after more than four decades of ESOPs, there is a great deal of information and experience to learn from. The NCEO's *ESOP Communications Sourcebook*,[1] for instance, contains dozens of templates companies can use, developed by the NCEO and by over two dozen companies that have shared their best practices with us.

This chapter looks at two aspects of communications: what the law requires you must communicate, and what you can do to help employees understand and be engaged by the ESOP.

What You Have to Communicate

Federal law requires companies with ESOPs to make a number of reports to ESOP participants, and your company's top communications priority, of course, is to do everything the law requires. That includes the following items.

---

1. Corey Rosen et al., *The ESOP Company Board Handbook* (NCEO, 2014) (see nceo.org/r/sourcebook).

Announcing the Plan

When a plan is first adopted, participants must be notified before the end of the first plan year that a new plan is in place. There are no specific guidelines as to the content of this notice. The section later in this chapter on introducing the ESOP provides ideas on how to do this.

Annual Benefit Statement

On an ongoing basis, the most basic disclosure requirement is to provide a statement of benefits to participants. The statement must include at least the participant's accrued benefit (in a defined contribution plan such as an ESOP, that means account balances), a statement of vested benefits and/or a statement of when benefits will become vested, and a description of the information used to compute benefit accruals. If your plan is a KSOP (a combined 401(k) plan and ESOP) or allows employees to invest their own assets in company stock in the ESOP, then quarterly statements are required.

The minimal requirement here is simply to provide a statement, but successful companies often make the annual benefit statement the centerpiece of an educational effort. The statements bring together several of the key aspects of ownership education and take them to a personal level for each ESOP participant. To understand the statement, participants need to know where the stock price comes from, what vesting means, how allocations work, what forfeitures are, and how the stock and other investment accounts fit together.

Benefit statements provide a once-a-year opportunity when people focus more sharply on the ESOP than at any other time. John Ossa, a former president of ESOP-owned Gardeners Guild, says that the week leading up to the account statements is like standing at the bank window watching the teller count out your cash: "nothing's going to make you lose focus." Consider giving people a head start by engaging their thinking about valuation ahead of time. Some companies hold a "guess the stock price" contest, and others hold brown-bag meetings to discuss the valuation process.

Benefit statements can read like a foreign language. Rewrite them if you can to make them as intuitive and in plain English as possible, or borrow a trick from other companies and make the statement look like a stock certificate. If none of that is possible, consider providing an annotated statement. Take a fictional statement and draw circles and arrows to explain what the different parts mean. You can include this in a PowerPoint presentation, post it on a bulletin board, or make it interactive on an intranet site.

Summary Annual Report

The plan administrator must also furnish a summary annual report (SAR) each year to all participants or beneficiaries receiving benefits under the plan. The SAR is a brief summary of the activity of the plan (essentially a summary of key points in your Form 5500 filing) and must be presented in a form provided by the Department of Labor (DOL) regulations. The report, normally provided by your plan administrator, will include the following:

1. Plan expenses, including benefits paid out
2. Number of participants
3. Value of plan assets and change from prior year
4. Plan income for the year, including the employer contributions
5. Notice of participant rights to key additional information (accountant's report, more financial details, description of assets, and transactions that are over 54% of the plan asset value) or, alternatively, the full Form 5500 filing (employees can already obtain this from the DOL's own website or sites like www.FreeErisa.com)

The report can be distributed electronically if participants have ready access to devices that receive these reports. The complexity and formal requirements of an SAR mean it is unlikely to be a useful communications device.

Summary Plan Description

The required contents of the summary plan description (SPD) are detailed in DOL regulations. Generally, your attorney will prepare the SPD, but the law requires the document be written so that a typical employee can understand it. Plan administrators should review the SPD and try to make it as user-friendly as possible.

Several things must be in the SPD:

1. Employee rights under the plan
2. The name and contact information of the trustee
3. How assets are valued
4. What form the distribution will take (stock or cash)
5. The tax consequences and investment alternatives for the distribution
6. How and when employees will get their shares
7. Voting rights
8. How to file complaints

The administrator must furnish an SPD within 90 days of the date a person becomes an ESOP participant or beneficiary receiving benefits under the plan or, if later, within 120 days of the date the plan first becomes subject to Title I of ERISA (generally the date the IRS first issues a favorable determination letter related to the plan). The SPD must be revised and issued every five years if there have been material amendments to the plan, or every 10 years in any case. Whenever a material amendment is made to the plan, a Summary of Material Modification (SMM) must be provided to all participants no later than 210 days following the end of the year in which the modification became effective.

Companies with strong ESOP communications programs take different approaches to the SPD. Some prepare a standard, no-frills SPD to meet legal requirements and encourage people to pay more attention to other educational materials. Others create simple, short explanations of the SPD, making clear that the explanation is not a legal document and the formal SPD is what people should rely on if there is a conflict. Still other companies work hard to make the SPD itself an effective communications tool. The legal restrictions on the content of the SPD make it challenging to modify, but some companies have succeeded remarkably.

If you have a significant number of non-English speakers, translating the SPD or similar documents into their language is vital (also see the section "Non-English Speakers" below).

Communications on Distributions

When distributions are to be made from the plan, there are several legally required disclosure and communication responsibilities. The administrator must provide qualifying terminated participants with an opportunity to direct "eligible rollover distributions" to be transferred directly to a successor qualified plan or individual retirement account (IRA). Where the distribution exceeds $5,000 in value (or a lower amount if that is specified in the plan document), the administrator must notify the terminated participants of their right to defer distribution until normal retirement age.

Generally, where a terminated participant is eligible for a distribution of benefits from an ESOP, the administrator must give the participant the right to receive benefits distributed in the form of company stock and must notify him or her of restrictions on transfer and the right to require the company to repurchase the shares. It must also indicate what benefits are available if the employee dies before a certain date. A discussion of the tax treatment of the distribution must be included as well. If the company is an S corporation or if it is a C corporation the bylaws of which restrict ownership of all or substantially all of the stock of the company to the current employees or an ERISA trust, the requirement to offer distributions in company stock may be avoided. Banks that are not publicly traded and that are not allowed to buy back their own securities may avoid providing a put option for distributed stock if the participants can choose to take their distributions in cash.

The Pension Protection Act of 2006 added the requirement that certain items be included on the benefit statements, including an identification of the DOL's website so that participants can seek guidance on the legal standard for vesting and diversification. The Act further permits the distribution of the mandated statements to be in electronic as well as written form. This option may allow plan administrators to save both printing and mailing costs.

Diversification Rights

Where an ESOP has been in existence for 10 years or more, the administrator will also have a responsibility to notify participants about their right to diversify a portion of their account balances (generally 25% of their company stock account when the requirement kicks in, increasing to 50% of the stock account balance by the sixth year) by either receiving an in-service distribution or directing the investment into other investments within the trust, if the ESOP offers diversification internally. Where employees can direct their investments pursuant to diversification, they must receive a quarterly notice advising them of the benefits of diversification strategies in their portfolios.

Qualified Domestic Relations Orders

Finally, if a qualified domestic relations order (QDRO) is received by the company, information about it must be sent to the affected parties, along with applicable procedures and whether the order is qualified. QDROs are issued, usually in the case of a divorce, to direct part of a former participant's benefit to another person, usually the former spouse.

Non-English Speakers

If you have fewer than 100 participants and 25% or more are literate only in the same foreign language, or if you have 100 or more participants and the lesser of 500 participants or 10% of the participants are literate only in the same foreign language, you must tell them how they can get help understanding the SPD, annual report, account statement, and other key material. The notice must be in the relevant language.

Some Things You Do Not Have to Communicate

This list could go on and on, of course, but here are some of the most important things you do not need to communicate (but are not prevented from sharing):

1. Employee salaries, either for specific people or in aggregate
2. Company financial information
3. A copy of the valuation report

4. Minutes of board or fiduciary meetings
5. Results of shareholder votes
6. Offers to buy the company
7. Deliberations about whether to set up or change the ESOP
8. Reasons for making changes in the plan
9. Names of people selling stock to the ESOP
10. Individual share holdings, in or outside the plan, including share rights, such as stock options
11. Statement of investment risk or other material that might appear in a tender offer

Basic Things You Should Communicate

In addition to the legally required material, any effective communications policy should communicate at least the four additional items listed below:

1. *Why the company adopted an ESOP.* Why did your company set up the plan and, if you change it, why did you change it? Talk about the alternatives the company/seller had and the advantages and disadvantages of each. Don't shy away from noting the benefits to a founder or to the company as a reason. Openness on these topics makes all your other communication more effective. Often the seller or senior manager is the best person to deliver this message.

2. *ESOP basics.* Even if you do not plan to invest in broad ESOP education, employees do need to hear some of the basics: when they become participants, what they need to do to receive an allocation, how vesting works, etc.

3. *Frequently asked questions.* Set up an online FAQ or distribute a physical booklet. Many companies set up an ESOP committee, or direct a member of the HR department, to gather real questions, research the answers, and share them with the work force.

4. *Company information.* At least some basic information on how the company is doing financially and what its goals are should be shared widely.

Beyond the Basics: Ongoing Communications Best Practices

Some companies just stop at the basics and figure they have fulfilled their responsibility to employees. They may believe that benefits of the ESOP will sell themselves over time. Good luck with that. What will really happen is that people will file their SPD and other documents somewhere and forget about the ESOP. What they will learn about the ESOP will mostly be what other employees tell them. If you want an effective and sustainable ESOP, you need to make communications an ongoing process. Not only will this make sure people understand the plan and its benefits, but the very fact of receiving frequent communications itself sends an important message about the importance of the ESOP.

The final section of this chapter provides examples of how companies have communicated effectively, but first let us look at how to communicate. There are some basic principles of communication:

- Focus on the three stages of learning (attributed to Ben Franklin and a lot of other people):
    1. Tell me and I forget
    2. Teach me and I learn
    3. Involve me and I remember
- Unlearn when needed. As baseball legend Satchel Paige said, "it ain't what you know that hurts you; it's what you know that just ain't so."
- When explaining an ESOP, remember it is hard to remember what you didn't once know either.
- Different people learn differently, so use different communication tools.
- Explain, don't sell.

"Tell Me" Communications

Annual meetings, newsletters, written documents, and even FAQs are examples of "tell me" communications. There are two tricky issues here. First, what we hear and what is said are not always the same. People put what they hear or read into some contextual framework they have about what things like ownership and retirement planning mean. That may shift the meaning away from what you intend. Second, memory is a very complicated process. Much of what we learn in tell-me communications will soon be forgotten. Chip and Dan Heath in their insightful book *Made to Stick* suggest six keys to making communications more memorable. Communications should be:

- *Succinct:* Too much information all at once is hard to absorb. Use smaller more frequent communications.
- *Unexpected:* We remember unexpected things much better, so highlight what is unexpected in an ESOP. For instance, you can emphasize that employee ownership does not mean employees actually buy stock.
- *Concrete:* Use as many specific examples as possible. Use number-based examples whenever possible.
- *Credible:* Although communications from colleagues may be more credible in explaining how an ESOP works, top leadership must be involved to explain why there is an ESOP.
- *Emotional:* Try to link explaining ownership to what it means to be an owner day to day. You can, for instance, ask people to imagine how they might feel differently about coming to work as an owner.
- *Stories:* This is the most important point. We remember stories far better than more abstract explanations. Having former employees talk about what an ESOP meant to them (or, if you are new, asking a nearby ESOP company to send some of its employee-owners to talk about what an ESOP means to them) will be much more memorable.

I would add "frequent" to this list. Sending out frequent communications is itself an important communication about the importance of the ESOP.

"Teach Me" Communications

Teach me communications are about learning. They involve people not just absorbing information, but thinking about it. There are lots of teach-me kinds of communications. Most involve some kind of live presentation. The best ones ask people to learn interactively. For instance, rather than just present the annual valuation report, have employees first break up into groups and guess what the number will be and why it would have changed. It doesn't matter what they come up with; it matters that they have been thinking about it and thus are more primed to hear the actual explanation. To get people to ask questions, require that everyone come to the meeting having written one down first. That makes everyone think at least a little about what they are about to hear.

"Involve Me" Communications

We never learn anything as well as when we have to use it. "Involve me" communications ask people to put the information to use. One of the best ways to do that is to train a group of people to explain some aspect of an ESOP or the company's financials then have them explain it to other people. You never learn anything as well as when you have to explain it to someone else. Role-playing about how an ESOP works is another good technique. Other involve-me ideas include playing some game (Jeopardy is popular) to get people to think about ESOPs. Employees can also write for the newsletter, post FAQs, serve as ESOP mentors to new employees, and even be on ESOP communications committees.

What-You-Know-That-Just-Ain't-So Problems

Part of effective ESOP communication is finding out what people assume about ESOPs that isn't true. They may know someone who was in a great ESOP or a lousy one, and that may color their view. Employees often believe that the ESOP is just a tax dodge for owners, that the company can just continue as it is without being sold, that they will never get their money, that the valuation is just a made-up number, that executives get way overpaid, and much more. Focus groups can be a great way to ferret out these beliefs. People will open up more in these groups if you ask what they think others get wrong about ESOPs.

Remember What You Once Did Not Know

I started professional life as a college teacher. In my lectures to students, I used words like "correlation" that were by then second-nature to me but that students did not really understand. Of course, I once didn't know either. But it is hard to remember what you once did not know, which is why experts like lawyers can have a hard time communicating in a language people grasp. It takes a conscious effort to think about every specialized word or concept you use, but after a while, it too can become second nature.

Use Different Ways to Learn

Some people learn more from visuals, others from meetings, from reading, from FAQs, and so on. So use different media approaches as much as possible.

Explain, Don't Sell

Don't try to sell the plan. Employees consistently comment negatively on presentations peppered with cheerleading. Explanations should cover risks and rewards of the new plan. The explanations should also include the legal rights employees have as ESOP participants. Explain why the company chose to implement the ESOP. Employees will not believe an argument solely highlighting potential benefits to employees. Be open about the tax and planning benefits to the seller. On the other hand, many sellers choose an ESOP over other routes for liquidity because of a genuine concern about their legacy and the employees. That should be explained too, as well as what the alternatives would have been if the sale were not made to the ESOP. Employees will arrive at their own conclusions if not overtly informed of the company's motive for implementing a plan. Most of the time, employees will understand the reason behind an ownership plan if it is clearly explained.

Best Practices from ESOP Companies on ESOP Communications Strategies

The following section describes ideas from ESOP companies that the companies have found particularly successful. You can see actual examples of what companies do in the NCEO's *ESOP Communications*

Sourcebook, which includes a CD with handouts, presentations, and other media from a variety of ESOP companies.

ESOP Communications Committees

The best communications programs almost always involve creating an ESOP communications committee made up of employees to design and run the program.

For example, Walman Optical, a Minneapolis company, has an ESOP communications committee consisting of interested nonmanagement employees. It has an impressive list of accomplishments and resources: a front-line finance program (based on an NCEO curriculum), frequent social events, an employee manual, a mentorship program, and presentations. One reason the committee keeps up so many activities is that it sets high expectations for new members. Prospective members of the committee see a detailed job description so they know that they will be expected to work, some of it on their own time. "No one thinks it's just a lunch and a chat," said human resources (HR) director Missy McManigle.

Another company, Holden Industries, developed an ESOP communications committee to actively participate in employee communication and education around ownership. Divisional presidents nominated employees to serve on the committee along with members of the HR team that worked on the pre-transaction employee communications. The committee's inaugural year "was a learning experience," said HR director Barbara Barkley. She and executive vice president Art Miller attribute some of the committee's challenges to the presence of HR representatives on the team. "Staff often deferred to [the expertise] of HR on what to do," Barkley explained. Instead of creating an atmosphere of collaboration and idea generation, this structure made it difficult for committee members to openly voice their opinions. As a result, Holden tried something different. The HR representatives stepped down, and employees would no longer be appointed to the committee. Service on the committee is now voluntary, and employees submit an application comprised of a short essay explaining why they would like to serve on the committee. The committee still partners with the HR department to plan event and activity logistics.

The Initial Meeting

Announcing a new plan to employees is a major opportunity. An employee ownership plan may replace or change contributions to another plan. After a company has spent time explaining the original plan's virtues, it must now explain why the new plan is superior. If a preexisting plan, such as a 401(k), is being eliminated or, more commonly, company contributions to it are being reduced, many employees may be skeptical about the new ESOP, even if the company contributions to it will be higher. We tend to value things we have lost more than things we might gain, so this is a natural reaction.

Moreover, many ESOPs are set up to buy out an owner. This can be a confusing and sometimes worrisome situation for some employees. Some will wonder if this really is a benefit for them or just a way to give the departing owner a benefit, maybe at their expense somehow. Some employees will assume, even if told the opposite, they have to buy stock or make concessions. Some employees will worry about the future of the company after the seller leaves.

At the first meeting, explain the basics and save detailed explanations for future meetings. Employees will want to know what stock is, how it is valued, how they can cash in their shares, how much the company will put into the plan, the risks involved, allocation and vesting rules, and the rights of ownership. At this first meeting, focus then on the basics: what do I get, when do I get it, and how much might it be worth. When planning the meeting to announce the ESOP, think about who ought to deliver which messages. Having key leaders speak and directly address their motivations and hopes for the ESOP can be invaluable. Other messages, such as the background about ESOPs, their limitations, and their potential advantages, may be best delivered by an outsider, who is more likely to be seen as impartial.

When Harpoon Ale set up an ESOP to buy 48% of the company, it gathered all 187 employees together to announce the plan. It issued a press release and sent photos of the meeting to reporters, generating a lot of coverage and providing employees a sense that this was an unusual and big step for a company. Then it went a step further. It sent employees to other ESOP companies, like Web Industries, to learn more about their experience with ESOPs. Employees were so impressed that they decided to offer free beer to anyone who came to the company store who worked for an employee-owned company.

Follow-Up Meetings

After the initial meeting, hold periodic follow-up meetings. Ongoing ESOP explanations should be held periodically, often as part of some other company or staff meeting. A good strategy is to take a particular aspect of ESOPs, such as vesting and allocation rules or plan distribution rules, and explain just that piece. It is a lot easier to absorb small bites of information, and the frequency of discussions communicate in another important way: they remind people that the ESOP is an important part of the company culture.

Orientation meetings are also an essential component. Most companies have employee orientation programs to explain job responsibilities. These programs focus on job training and communicating company policies, procedures, and expectations. Employee ownership companies must also provide orientation covering ownership plans and company culture. This can be especially important—and difficult—for individuals joining employee ownership companies. Their new rights and responsibilities involve new skills and a new understanding of their roles as employees. Creating an ownership orientation program is critical. While programs differ from firm to firm, they usually include the following elements: orientation materials, mentoring, and presentations.

Perhaps the most developed—and imitated—orientation program is that of Web Industries, an ESOP company that converts materials for manufacturers. Rather than having managers orient new employees, Web Industries has existing employees assume this role. A four-week training program includes 16 one-hour sessions on corporate history, ownership structure, teamwork, safety, work-order processing, benefits, math, customer service, and continuing improvement. The sessions move over the weeks from lectures to a discussion format as new employees acclimate. Bimba Manufacturing runs a similar orientation program with employees leading ESOP classes.

Calibre Systems, a 700-employee 100% ESOP technology consulting company in Alexandria, Virginia, developed a five-year cycle of how it shares information. There is a specific plan for what information will be shared and when, including periodic orientation sessions for new employees and those wanting a refresher. There is an ongoing set of other programs, including celebrations, intranet resources, recognition events, company information packages and news, ESOP basics and updates, and more. The system provides multiple touchpoints for the ESOP and the company. Critically, Calibre also does a periodic employee survey (in this case the NCEO's ownership culture survey) to see how it is doing and what needs improvement.

Employees as Trainers: Mentoring and Teaching

Mentoring can be crucial to employee orientation. Burns and McDonnell, a large employee-owned engineering firm, has one of the most developed mentoring programs. Here, management-appointed mentors attend classes and then serve for one year. They also participate in performance appraisals of their "protégés." Mentors assist new employees with goal setting, training, communicating ownership culture, and teaching new employees about the company.

At W.L. Gore & Associates, the employee-owned manufacturer of Gore-Tex, new employees are assigned "sponsors." There may be one or more sponsors per employee. Sponsors take on all standard mentoring roles and act as the employee's evaluator and advocate. A sponsor helps ensure that new employees get started on their jobs, that they receive credit for their contributions, and that they are compensated fairly. When employees move on to new responsibilities, new sponsors are assigned to them.

Many ESOP companies, such as the employee-owned Braas Company, train employees to teach ESOP classes. Employees instructing classes, for the first time for many of them, may lack a professional's polish and presentation skills. This is more than offset, however, by the greater enthusiasm and credibility employees bring to this process.

In each of these examples, employees themselves assume responsibility for orientations. This is part of company culture, and it provides an initial and powerful symbol to new workers that employee involvement is the norm. Having employees drive the communications process also adds credibility. Finally, and perhaps most importantly, it provides an exceptional learning opportunity for existing employees. The best way to learn a subject is by teaching it; no one is as proud of a company as when explaining it to someone else. Even if new workers do not need training, this alone would justify an orientation program. Some companies even give employees cards reading "CEO"—Certified Employee Owner.

Newsletters

Newsletters are a common form of corporate communications. Many focus on news about individual employees. They can also provide an educational forum. For instance, Woodward Communications, an employee-owned media company in Iowa, focuses its newsletter on quality issues, the ESOP, company news, and other corporate topics. Newsletters normally should be printed and distributed. One good idea is to mail them to the employee's home, where they might get more attention and even spark discussion with a spouse. If employees are all regular Web users, an electronic newsletter might work, but even regular Web users are less likely to read this online than something printed.

One of the best ways to use newsletters is to make sure employees participate in writing it or contributing materials to it. That sense of ownership will make it much more salient to more people.

Intranets

A secure intranet site allows a company to disseminate important elements of its corporate culture widely and frequently every time an employee uses the network. It can also be used for many different business applications, including sales and marketing, human resources, operations, and collaborative work processes such as cross-company discussion sessions.

If a company decides to set up an intranet, it must ensure that all employees have access to information. Achieving universal access is a challenge in most businesses, particularly those with employees whose jobs traditionally do not require computer use. If all employees do not have access, the intranet's impact will be minimal. There are practical ways to provide widespread computer access. For example, computer terminals, or "kiosks," can be placed in highly accessible areas on shop floors, in break rooms, or in other common areas. Each kiosk would consist of a networked personal computer, a mouse, and a screen. Ideally, a ratio of one computer per ten employees should be the goal. With email, discussion groups, and information searching and retrieval, this ratio would reduce downtime resulting from employees waiting for a busy computer to become available.

Intranet sites commonly have an explanation of the ESOP, FAQs, stories about the company and employees, and examples of employees leaving with plan distributions. Some contain interactive tools, such as a way for employees to project future account values under various realistic scenarios. As with newsletters, employee involvement in creating and maintaining the site will increase its use and relevancy.

Social Media

More and more ESOP companies now use social media to communicate about the company and the ESOP. Videos of company events, explanations of the ESOP by a company leader, even employee-written songs about the ESOP are now being posted to YouTube. Twitter can be used for quick updates or "did you know" factoids about the company and the plan. Chances are, you have a number of employees who are active social media users. Get them involved in figuring out what strategies will work.

Employee Ownership Month

Since 1987, October has been Employee Ownership Month. Companies have used this opportunity to organize events and refocus on communications strategies pertaining to employee ownership. An effective way to plan for Employee Ownership Month is to launch a committee composed of nonmanagement employee-owners, or mobilize an existing one, to organize the month's events. This group should meet on company time, be given a budget, and, most of all, be encouraged to innovate; these measures will maximize commitment. After all, Employee Ownership Month should be a celebration, and the goal should be to have fun.

Employee Ownership Month events are limited only by imagination. Some companies have used trivia contests and running races, for example. If your company is feeling ambitious, it can plan a month-long celebration with different weekly events. For example, you can kick off the celebration by catering a meal or holding a potluck dinner. The second week can be reserved for an open house and facility tour, a visit from an elected official, or a media event planned around the signing of a proclamation. In the third week, hold a shareholders' meeting, and in the fourth week, have educational sessions and roundtable meetings that consist of sharing financial information. Lastly, you can wrap up Employee Ownership Month with a banquet, where awards are distributed to employees who offer ideas about ownership culture, for instance. Or, more casually, hold a picnic with games.

First National Bank of Bemidji in Minnesota holds an annual dinner celebration as the highlight of its events. Most recently, it also posted signs at the bank and encouraged employees to talk to customers about being an ESOP. At the dinner, games were played around ESOP themes and employees in each department came up with skits that incorporated the idea of being employee owners.

Try to plan events that best suit your company's culture, work environment, and budget; events don't have to be extravagant or expensive to be fun and effective.

External Communications: Marketing Employee Ownership

One of the most effective things you can do to make the ESOP more salient to employees is to market being employee-owned to suppliers, customers, the media, and legislators. If employee ownership is stressed in company advertisements, marketing brochures, letterhead, and other materials, employees are regularly reminded that their company believes their contributions are important. Moreover, customers will be curious and will ask employees how they feel about being owners.

This can be, of course, a double-edged sword. If your employees are not happy about their ownership plan, no matter what the reason, they may react negatively to the advertisements and maybe even toward customers.

There are lots of ways to market being an ESOP company. Many companies give each employee a business card reading "Owner." That's a powerful tool for employee pride but can also create greater interest from customers. Your website can proudly and prominently say "Employee Owned" and have a page explaining it (the NCEO site www.esopinfo.org has useful infographics for this). You can put "Employee Owned" on your letterhead and vehicles and any other public-facing material. Jackson's Hardware in San Rafael, California, puts a two-page ad in the local paper during Employee Ownership Month with pictures and years of service for all its 70 or so employees.

Open Houses, Receptions, and Tours

An open house is a great excuse to invite families, civic leaders, and local business leaders to the company; here, employee-owners can give tours and facilitate the event. An event like this can be an easy way to reinforce the company's commitment to employee ownership and keep participation active. It's especially important to invite your congressional representatives to these open houses.

Getting in the News

Everyone likes recognition. One of the most effective communication methods is a media event inviting reporters to write about your company and employee ownership. Your company can produce television commercials and/or radio spots, place ads in the local newspaper, or issue press releases to your local media about Employee Ownership Month. (We've found that some of the best venues for these types of stories are within industry-specific trade publications.)

Branding

Many of these activities can be lumped under the concept of branding. Perhaps no company has brought that all together as well as North Highland, a 100% ESOP-owned company that provides management and technology consulting services. It involved employees at all levels to develop an integrated employee ownership branding strategy. The result was a branding motto, "Own your life. Own your career. Own your company." This brand permeates all major processes at North Highland, including employee recruitment, policy and benefit evaluation, employee communications, marketing, and training. Employee-owners have a ready answer for what makes their company different.

Conclusion

Effective communications is a lot of hard work. To work well, it requires active involvement of employees at multiple levels. But you are spending a lot of money on your ESOP. You wouldn't buy an expensive new car and then not maintain it. If you want the ESOP to work, the time will be well worth spending.

KEY TAKEAWAYS

- Work with your plan administrator to make sure you regularly communicate what the law requires.
- Remember that documents prepared by lawyers and other specialists are written for specific legal purposes and will be hard for people to understand, so provide additional material that is simpler.
- "Tell me" communications such as newsletters, presentations, brochures, annual statements, FAQs, e-mail updates, etc., are an essential base for communication, but much of that information will not be remembered (or often even read).
- "Teach me" communications such as meetings with time for lots of questions and small training sessions taught by other employees will help people understand how the plan works, but employees won't necessarily integrate that knowledge into their day-to-day thinking.
- "Involve me" communications, such as train-the-trainer programs, playing games based on ESOP issues, having people guess the ESOP valuation, etc., will help people truly understand what the ESOP does.
- Orienting new employees to the ESOP is essential, but remember to offer refresher courses to existing employees.
- Get employees involved in developing and delivering communications material.
- Market yourself as employee-owned; it helps your brand and makes employee ownership more real to employees.

Chapter 9

Creating and Growing an Ownership Culture

Back in the 1980s, Phelps County Bank adopted an ESOP, which owned a minority of the stock. It was a good benefit for people, but Emma Lou Brent, the new CEO of the company, wasn't happy. The ESOP just was not doing much for the company. The bank was doing all right, but employees were not really acting like owners. I went out to visit Emma in Rolla, Missouri, and told her about what the research showed about what makes ESOPs work: "You need to be sure the plan is financially meaningful and well explained, but the real key is to find ways to get employees involved as owners in generating ideas. Hard work is great, but what really makes a company succeed are lots of new ideas."

Emma, who later became head of the state community bank association, grabbed on to that idea and energetically set out to make it happen. I'll talk about the specific approach the bank used later, but over the next few years, Phelps became an idea machine. Emma saw to it that all employees went to bank management training because, in her view, they all were business people. Employees got excited. Two national banks moved into town and took over local operations. Phelps and its employees ate their lunch. Phelps has remained consistently high-performing, and employees, most of whom stay around a long time, leave with account balances well into six figures. A couple who shared a janitorial job for 15 years left with enough money to buy a very nice new home.

Just about every ESOP company wants to have employees who think and act like the employee-owners at Phelps. Compelling research and decades of experience show that employee ownership is in fact a powerful tool to improve corporate performance—but only when companies have cultures in which employees think and act like owners. That is a lot more than being nice to customers, cutting down on waste, coming to work on time, and even working hard on the job. An effective ownership culture, the research shows, is one that generates lots of ideas. Most of these ideas are small improvements that cumulatively add up to much stronger performance, and a few are big ideas that lead to major new initiatives.

Companies that have these high-involvement, idea-generating systems, the research shows, generate an incremental 6% to 11% added growth per year over what their prior performance relative to their industries would have predicted. For instance, if ABC Auto Parts was growing 2% faster per year relative to competitors before its ESOP, it would grow 8% to 13% per year faster. Companies with more traditional top-down systems actually show a *decline* in performance after their ESOP because they raised, but did not meet, employee expectations.

Creating an ownership culture involves at least these six elements:

1. Provide a financially meaningful ownership stake, enough to be an important part of employees' financial security.
2. Provide ownership education that teaches people how the company makes money and their role in making that happen.
3. Share performance data about how the company is doing overall and how each workgroup contributes to that.
4. Train people in business literacy so they understand the numbers the company shares.
5. Often (but not always) share profits through incentive plans, profit sharing, or other tools.
6. Build employee involvement not just by allowing employees to contribute ideas and information but by making that part of their everyday work through teams, feedback opportunities, devolution of authority, and other structures.

Why Ideas Matter

The still-common assumptions about effective employee ownership are that it motivates people to work harder (it can) and that people working harder will mean the company will make more money (it will, but not by much). There is nothing wrong with employees making more effort at work. The problem is that getting people to do the same job the same way with more effort does not actually produce a very significant result.

Simple math can show why. The first issue to determine is what percentage of your population will actually change behavior in response to an incentive. Every company has incorrigibles, people who just are not that engaged and won't be no matter what you do. That's obvious. But what is not obvious is that in addition to the incorrigibly bad, there are the incorrigibly good—the people who are working as hard as they can, thank you, and no added incentive can change that. Over the last 30 years or so, we at the NCEO have been asking company leaders what percentage of their workforce falls into each category, and the answer is usually that about half fall into one or the other, mostly because there are a lot of incorrigibly good employees.

The second issue is for how many minutes of the day will the people whose behavior might change actually work harder? Another 30 minutes a day? 15? Our respondents say 30 minutes would be terrific, if a stretch. So let's be optimistic and assume that can be achieved.

Finally, working harder will mostly only affect labor costs. It doesn't lower your rent, taxes, inventory (other than a small percentage for waste avoided), marketing and fuel costs, etc. Labor's percentage of total costs varies a lot, but is commonly 30% or less, especially in manufacturing, where extra effort (as opposed to better ideas) really matters most.

So now multiply 0.5 (the percentage of the workforce whose behavior changes) x .067 (the extra time worked in a day) x 0.3 (the percentage of labor costs). Impressed? That's a 1.2% reduction in costs, assuming (a big assumption) that your incentive plan is a slam-bang success. Chances are, it will be a lot less than that.

So if getting people to work harder at the same tasks won't get you very far down the road, what can greater employee engagement get you? As study after study has shown, it is employees coming up with lots of new ideas that really make the difference (see *Ideas Are Free* by Dean Schroder and Alan Robinson for a persuasive review of these studies). Getting people to do this takes a lot more than a carrot, the research shows, and far more than "open-door" policies (every company has one of these, but few people ever darken the managers' doors). It requires an organizational culture based on teams at all levels with real power and lots of information to make decisions about their work. Hypertherm, a

100% ESOP-owned plasma cutting tool manufacturer with over 1,000 employees, generates over three ideas per employee per year and uses 90% of them. Competitors may be able to copy their cutting tools to one extent or another, but copying their culture is another matter.

Imagine if even some significant percentage of your work force were to see it as part of their job to come up with ideas, or maybe just share important information with people who would benefit from it (you may not always know how to turn off the gas, but it is still useful to tell someone it is leaking). At least some of these new ideas will lead to ways to save money, serve customers better, help people stay safer and healthier, find new markets or products, be more efficient, and lots more. At least some of this information will make it possible for other people to make far better decisions. And once your culture gets this ingrained, it can become viral, with even more people coming up with more ideas and sharing information about more things.

This chapter looks at what we at the NCEO have learned about how to get from here to there. Our webinars, annual conference, and annual Get the Most Out of Your ESOP meeting provide much more in-depth tools.

Step One: Open-Book Management

In 1983, Jack Stack and a group of 19 managers put up enough money to make a down payment on the purchase of the Springfield ReManufacturing Division of International Harvester (now Navistar). After asking 50 banks, they got a loan to buy the division that left them with an 89:1 debt-to-equity ratio. Soon after they bought the company, they set up an ESOP and issued it enough shares so that it owned about 35% of the company, thus making all 119 employees owners. The stock price was 10 cents per share.

The managers bought the company as a last-ditch effort to save it from closing. Stack knew they could not afford to lose even $10,000 in a month. He wanted everyone to understand that and to find ways to turn things around. The best way to do that, he decided, was to teach every employee, mostly high-school educated machine operators, how to read financial statements so they knew just what was at stake. These financial statements provided the high-level picture, but at the operational level, what mattered was a whole series of performance measures that were specific to each area of work (backlog, efficiency measures, waste, sales projections, etc.). There were usually one or two critical numbers that deserved special focus. So employees were taught to understand those as well.

Sharing all this information was radical enough in 1983, but Stack went a big step further. He wanted employees to learn to project the numbers and chart their progress against them, discussing the result in weekly "huddles" at each operational level. The operational huddles sent people to huddles for the whole company to do the same thing. These huddles provided the chance for employees to talk about ways to make the numbers better. They were also very motivating. Not tracking the numbers with employees, Stack said, was like a basketball coach not telling the players the score or any of the statistics about how individuals and the team were doing. Business was a great game, and people would like to play if they knew the score, could do something about it, and had a stake in the action.

Today, Springfield ReManufacturing has become SRC Holdings. It is now a 100% ESOP with over 1,200 employees in 17 businesses, on its way to over 2,000 employees in the next several years. Its stock has climbed to $435 per share in 2015 (adjusting for splits). Its system of management, the Great Game of Business, was laid out by Stack and his coauthor Bo Burlingham in a best-seller that was recently reissued. SRC has a whole division to teach the Game to other companies and holds a large annual conference on the idea.

Stack is not the only ESOP company leader to practice open-book management. In fact, most ESOP companies share the numbers in some way. But the best systems all have a few key traits in common:

- They share income statements, balance sheets, and cash flow statements, but use them more as an overall scorecard than a guide to action.
- They develop localized measures of performance, often with input from employees, that are highly visible and regularly tracked.
- Employees meet in groups periodically to come up with ideas on how to improve performance as measured by these performance numbers.

- Employees get the training they need to make their work more effective.

To do this right is a lot of work, but companies that encourage more employee involvement in decisions but then don't provide them with the information and tools to make these decisions in a way that makes business sense will simply get a lot more bad decisions.

Sharing Income Statements and Balance Sheets

Most ESOP companies share at least some information from income statements and balance sheets. Some share cash flow statements as well. For most people, these numbers have a largely symbolic value. They do not provide any clear idea of what to do other than try harder. That symbolism is critical, however, because sharing these numbers is a clear message that people are really owners.

It makes sense to share these numbers at an annual meeting if at all possible. Periodic updates can be shared as well. In general, going into great detail has little value because most of these details cannot be acted on. Instead, focus on a few key issues and explain what they are and why they matter. Then look at those items that represent significant variance, good or bad, and explain what that is about and what can be done about it.

It is essential to provide some basic training to help people understand the numbers. The NCEO's *ESOP Communications Sourcebook*[1] has ideas and templates for this. Some companies have actual classes on understanding the numbers. Others have someone good at explaining the numbers in simple terms do that at the meeting. Still others have employees explain the numbers. In the most developed (and I would say the best) approach, companies train employees to be "certified employee owners (CEOs)," employees who learn about all the key ESOP and company issues. They then train other employees to be CEOs. These programs work so well because there is no better way to learn something than to have to explain it to someone else.

---

1. Paul Horn et al., *The ESOP Communications Sourcebook,* 6th ed. (NCEO, 2014) (see nceo.org/r/sourcebook).

Sharing Critical Numbers

At Barclay Water Management in Boston, about half the workforce sells water treatment services for boiler and building environmental control applications. Before the company adopted an ESOP, salespeople sold fixed-price service contracts to provide the needed consultation and chemicals. Commissions were based on sales. Salespeople had an incentive to make customers happy, even if it meant adding services, such as FedEx shipping of chemicals. After Barclay adopted an ESOP, it switched to basing the bonus on the contribution to overhead and profits. The numbers were posted online in an interface that updated in real time every time a service contract was changed. Salespeople, for instance, now asked customers if they really needed overnight delivery. They also asked about other services Barclay could provide, such as cleaning ice machines (a source of considerable contamination) and testing and treating potable water for salmonella and other dangerous bacteria. These services were low-cost but high-margin.

All salespeople could see all the numbers for everyone, making it easier to test performance. In the next year, salespeople were more careful about how they serviced their customers and started looking for adjunct services to provide. A soft economy kept sales flat, but profits tripled as the way customers were serviced changed. Customer retention remained at a very high level, showing that many of the services formerly given away to keep customers happy (such as FedEx shipping of chemicals) were things that did not need to be done. In the next few years, the adjunct services started to grow very quickly, and the technical people got to work to develop proprietary systems for environmental controls, which became the highest-margin part of the business.

Every company has different critical numbers. Ideally, management and nonmanagement employees work together to identify what they are and how best they can be tracked and used.

Once the critical numbers are identified, the next step is to structure employee involvement systems so that people can put these to good use to help the company move forward. That process is described next.

Step Two: Employee Involvement

Some companies already have a robust employee involvement culture in place when they start their ESOP, but most start out more traditionally run. It can be a long leap to get to a high-involvement culture, a leap that usually requires several interim steps. Because it is often a major change, don't get discouraged by the missteps you will take along the way. The process will take considerable time and commitment to become effective.

Why Open Doors Are Not Enough

So where can you start? How about that old reliable, the open-door policy? Does your company have an "open-door" policy? Chances are it does. In fact, do you know any companies with official "closed-door" policies? The truth is, almost every company says it has an open-door policy. The problem is that not many people walk through that door. To be sure, some open-door policies are mere rhetoric. Management really doesn't expect employees to stand at their door, wouldn't have the time for them if they did, and wouldn't know exactly what to do with what the employees suggested anyway. But it sounds good. Even where these policies are sincere and management really does expect employees to take advantage of their genuine interest in employee ideas, unfortunately, very few employees walk through the door. It is hard for employees to know when it is OK to stop working, knock on the open door, and confidently express an idea to a boss. Even if they do all that, many bosses won't have the time to really think the idea through and are likely to reject all but the obviously no-brainer ideas out of hand.

For all these reasons, open-door policies are very rarely enough to create a genuinely participative environment in which employees feel not just that they can share ideas and information but that it is part of their job to do so. The key is to not just allow employee participation but structure it into work routines and expect it as part of everyone's job requirements. Participation is not just a right of ownership; it is a responsibility as well.

The difficulty with open-door policies may explain a persistent finding in research on employee attitudes toward ownership cultures. When management is asked how participative the company is, it consistently provides significantly higher ratings than employees do on the same questions. In management's mind, they know that they genuinely welcome employee involvement. Employees, however, see a more ambiguous message. Remember that for the large majority of employees, participation is a new experience. Few employees have had experience in a participative workplace before their own employer became employee-owned. School and family are usually not highly participative either. Almost no employee has been trained in such skills as team-based problem solving or how to present ideas effectively.

Open-door policies should not be abandoned, however, even if they are not in and of themselves enough. When employees do walk through an open door, a few practices can help make this opportunity more useful. First, if managers are often tied up in meetings or other tasks, make sure there are times when management is specifically available for employees. It's not unlike college professors posting office hours. Second, make sure that any suggestions result either in a detailed explanation of why the idea might not work or, if further consideration is needed, exactly what will happen next and when—and then follow through. Third, it makes sense to try to find something in the idea that is worth pursuing, even if it is just a piece of the proposal. Finally, managers should not assume that management always knows best. It's worth taking a risk on some ideas management does not agree with, even just to show that employee ideas are taken seriously.

Suggestion Systems

Next up on the old reliable—but usually not very effective—list are suggestion systems. As one wag put it, "any company that uses a suggestion box to get employee suggestions needs suggestions about how to get suggestions." But suggestion systems don't have to be just a largely symbolic—and ineffective—tool. Several key principles can help them work better:

- *You don't have to propose the solution.* One of the biggest barriers to making a suggestion system work is the nostrum "don't tell me the problem unless you know how to fix it." So if you smell gas leaking but don't know how to turn off the valve, don't bother me. If someone has heard a consistent complaint from customers but does not know how to fix the problem, do you really not want to know about it? So step one is to call the suggestion system something else, like the "idea box" or "feedback system" or "problem resolution process." Employees should be encouraged to submit items such as barriers to getting their work done better, ideas on how things could improve, or just useful tidbits of information ("the machine is running hotter than usual," or "there's a good source for data we use on the Internet").

- *You do need to think it through.* Suggestions dropped in the suggestion box often are ignored by management because they are intemperate ("how about cutting CEO pay?"), vague ("we need to communicate more"), or poorly thought out. A better approach is to create a suggestion form that asks for specific things to be included. For instance, the form might ask for the problem to be identified as specifically as possible, to show how it impedes work getting done, and ask for examples of how problems have arisen. If possible, employees can identify specific costs and solutions, but this is not a requirement. Ideally, a company should spend time teaching people how to think through issues so that they can do a cost analysis.

- *Provide a response, in writing, fast.* The number one reason employees tell us they become discouraged with employee-involvement efforts is a lack of feedback. Either ideas get no response at all, or the response comes weeks or months later. When a response does come, too often it is perfunctory ("we tried that before," or "we'll consider it") or patronizing ("your idea is greatly appreciated; we can't use it now, but we'll keep it on file"). What is really needed is a detailed written response that explains why the idea is being accepted, rejected, or passed on for further consideration. The response should be considered an opportunity to help educate employees about the nature of the business. In that sense, there are no bad submissions; every one provides a learning opportunity. Over time, the quality of suggestions will improve as a result.

- *Provide schedules for follow-up.* When an idea is going to be considered, the submitter should be told exactly what the process is. Who will consider it? When will a decision be made? If the process will take time, provide the submitter with updates. When a decision is made, let the submitter (and perhaps other employees) know. In some companies, the employee must actually sign off on the decision, indicating they are satisfied with it. Otherwise, the process is still open until a satisfactory resolution is reached.

- *Reward effort, not just success.* If submissions are used as an opportunity to teach people about business, then the volume of submissions may be as important as the quality. Moreover, as people learn more, their ideas will improve. There are also some people who will just throw out a lot of ideas. Many may not work, but a few may be very useful. Those people should be encouraged, not discouraged. After all, it does not take long to fill out a brief form explaining why an idea cannot be used. But how much might be gained from those one or two good ideas that actually work? The school grading model of idea evaluation—three good ideas out of ten is failing—doesn't work for business. Three out of ten is quite good. Even one out of ten may be great. One way to reward effort and outcome is to provide rewards for the best ideas but also to select, at random, a number of other submissions as well. A few companies even have a reward for the worst ideas.

Making Suggestion Systems Participative

Once you have taken these simple steps, a good way to get a process going is what Reflexite Corporation, a very successful ESOP company that eventually sold at a substantial multiple, first developed. They called it EARS (Employee Assistance Request System), but other companies have similar programs with their own names (Phelps County Bank called it Problem Busting Committees). We'll call it the Idea Factory.

The Idea Factory is essentially a way to create a participative suggestion process. Employees who have ideas, or identify a problem they do not know how to solve, fill out a form that asks them to identify the problem; indicate what it is costing in terms of time, waste, money, etc.; what ideas they have to address the problem (if any); and how much the ideas might cost in time of money. It is always OK to say "I don't know." Companies can and should develop more specific forms adapted to their businesses. All the submissions go to a steering committee that consists of both management and nonmanagement employees to act as the first screen.

Unless the problem can be quickly and easily resolved, the steering team creates a "corrective action team" (CAT), an ad hoc committee set up to solve the problem. The team has a coordinator, who may or may not be an expert in the subject matter, but whose charge it is to identify those people who are. People can also volunteer for the teams (all CATs are posted). Teams have a form they must fill out reporting on their progress. Almost all participants in CATs are non-management employees.

The teams make decisions about what to do about a problem and present it to the person who submitted it. A submission cannot be put to rest until the submitter agrees the problem has been resolved and signs off on it. Sometimes this process may take days; sometimes it can take months or longer.

The Idea Factory has five key elements that make it work so well:

1. It is highly visible, with all ideas being posted.
2. It identifies problems first, then finds solutions.
3. It has a high management priority.
4. It gets employees involved in solutions.
5. It requires that every request be resolved to the requester's satisfaction.

Phelps County Bank ran its problem-busting system for many years, but, over time, the employees became so used to forming teams on their own to solve problems—and management so accustomed to trusting their decisions—that now the process bypasses any formal committee and just runs on its own.

Team-Based Management

Creating employee teams is at the core of an ownership culture. They can be functional work area teams, cross-cutting teams (product development, safety, wellness, customer service, green practices, etc.), or ad-hoc teams that dissolve after solving specific problems. To make teams work, several key principles need to be followed:

- *Develop critical numbers.* For each function in a company, help employee groups develop critical cost analyses. What specific areas are causing cost problems? Is it excessive overtime use, customer returns, scrap, high phone bills, increasing postal rates, or energy consumption? How would a reduction of $1 in cost in any of these areas affect profits? How would driving down costs increase share prices? (Keep in mind that share prices are a multiple of earnings, so a dollar saved is not a dollar more in the stock price, it's several dollars more.) Red Dot, a Washington manufacturer, posts critical numbers in all work areas, and employees update them on a daily basis up against targets.

- *Map the process.* Have each group map its process for how decisions on spending money are made. Look at each step in the process and then ask people to think about how it can be done better. This may uncover unexpected issues. Maybe the office manager, for instance, is relying on only one supplier, or the truck drivers don't have a process for fuel monitoring. Flinchbaugh Engineering is one of many ESOP companies to use kaizen (continuous improvement) events to periodically rethink an entire process, getting everyone who touches the issue to get involved.

- *Create a mini-game.* Mini-games are short-term games employees in common function areas play to improve some specific number. The groups may be based on people's specific jobs (everyone in the warehouse, for instance) or common issues, such as safety or wellness. Management, or sometimes employees, isolate a particular challenge, such as improving on-time shipping, increasing the number of people getting health screening, saving energy, etc. People meet to share ideas on how to meet or exceed the challenge, then get a monetary or fun reward. SRC Holdings has been using mini-games for decades as a way for its teams to focus on a particular problem, usually with a 90-day target and a fun payout.

- *Create specific responsibilities and budgets.* Teams need a specific charge. What can they do and what can't they do? Who will be on them? Who will run them? How often will they meet? What are the rules for participation? Ambiguity about these things will make teams at best inefficient and at worst lead to their demise. Scot Forge, a very successful long-term 100% ESOP-owned company, started its teams without clear directions as to what they were supposed to do. Scot had very loyal employees who were eager to get involved, but were not sure what to do. Managers were inconsistent in how they responded to employee ideas as well. After about a year, Scot redesigned the teams with more specific tasks and responsibilities, and they became a very successful part of the company. No company takes this farther than W.L. Gore and Associates, the 10,000-employee manufacturer of Gore-Tex and lots of other high-tech products. There, any employee with an idea can form a team and draw down a budget without approval provided they can get enough other employees to join the team.

- *Get the right people.* Getting the right people on board is tricky. Should everyone affected be involved, such as a regular team meeting of the warehouse staff? That can help assure more buy-in and information sharing, but may be a waste of time for some people who do not have much to contribute. An alternative is "selective volunteering," where some people have to participate, but anyone who chooses to join the team can as well. That can leave out the more reticent people who may actually have some good ideas, however. Foldcraft, a 100% ESOP-owned manufacturer in Minnesota, puts all of its employees on self-forming, self-managing teams, allowing the teams to make sure they get the right people on board.

- *Train.* If employees are going to be making more decisions, they will make better ones if they are trained in how the company makes money and operates. Mayville Engineering, a 100% ESOP-owned company in Wisconsin, uses a combination of team meetings and one-on-one sessions to train workers to think critically about the work process and how to make improvements.

Programs Other Than Teams

Teams of all shapes and sizes are the most effective way to get employees to share ideas and information—and implement them—on a regular basis. But several companies have come up with other approaches that work to supplement their more ongoing structures.

Annual Meetings

Many companies have annual employee meetings, but only some of them turn these meetings into ways to generate ideas. New Belgium Brewery, a 100% ESOP-owned brewery that makes the iconic Fat Tire beer, holds an annual strategy retreat. Most of the employees work in Fort Collins, Colorado, but a significant number are elsewhere now that New Belgium distributes in over 25 states and has a brewery in Virginia. At the Annual Strategy Retreat, everyone comes back to Colorado. The meeting is part celebration, part review of the year and corporate strategy, and, importantly, part opportunity for all employees to identify one personal initiative that can help the company meet its strategic goal.

N-Link is a provider of technology services for government agencies. Its unique challenge is that almost all of its employees work on site at one agency or another. So each year, n-Link has a three-day retreat to bring people back together at a local resort. It's a fun weekend for employees and their families, but also a chance to go over the business results and strategy and let employees meet to come up with new ideas for moving forward.

Internet Solutions

SmithBucklin, a 700-employee ESOP-owned provider of membership, meeting, and other services to associations, created KnowledgeNet, an online repository launched in 2003 to allow employees to post and share ideas and best practices from their client work. That is common enough (albeit not as common as it could be, given the potential power of the tool). What is unusual at SmithBucklin is that the practices are peer-reviewed before being reused. An employee might, for instance, wonder about best practices for dealing with marketing a meeting, dealing with special food requests, or organizing a member database. Because all these issues have come up before, employees can quickly gain the benefit of the knowledge of other people at the firm.

Evaluating Your Participation Process

There are a lot of ways to get set up and periodically evaluate a participation process. The structure outlined below is based on some of the best practices the NCEO has observed from ESOP companies. To get started, management or (if there is one) an employee ownership steering committee should select what work areas of the company need more employee involvement, setting up workgroups by area. Employees from those areas should be invited to attend a meeting that will probably last 90 minutes or more. If a large number of employees is involved, a representative group should be designated (perhaps by selective volunteering, where people can voluntarily join the process, but some people who need to be involved are specifically asked to join). Ideally, each work area would be represented by about six to twelve employees.

Each team of employees would be asked to designate a group leader and recorder. The employees should then be given a handout asking them to discuss how to increase effective employee input into decisions affecting their work areas. They should be asked to decide (and record their decisions) on the following issues:

1. Who should be involved?
2. What is the scope of their authority (can they just make recommendations or can they actually make decisions on some or all issues)?
3. What specific issues can the group take up?
4. How can problems be identified for the group to consider? Can or should employees submit them on a form to the group? Should management be able to ask the group to address certain issues?
5. Is a budget needed? How much and what for?
6. Should people from outside their work area be involved in some or all meetings? If yes, who?
7. How will the meetings be run? Where? When? How often? Who will facilitate them?
8. Who will take the lead in organizing details of the process?
9. How will meetings, and their results, be communicated to other employees?
10. Should involvement be voluntary or mandatory?
11. Should meetings be on an ad hoc or regularly scheduled basis?
12. Who will measure effectiveness, and how will that be done?

13. What information will the group need to make good decisions?
14. How can the process be changed as people learn what works and what doesn't?

Have each group report back a synopsis of its discussion. Now re-examine the process with the entire group of participants to see what was effective and where improvements could have been made. Whether the participation effort was successful or not, there's something to be learned from analyzing it in this way. Management and/or the steering committee should then make the needed changes.

A Participation Checklist

A good tool is a participation checklist. That can then be mapped against what kind of decisions employees are involved in and/or should (or should not) be. The participation checklist in table 9-1 provides a template for doing that.

Employee Steering Committees

Many ESOP companies have an ESOP committee of some sort. Most of them focus on employee communication, training, and celebrations. These are all important roles. But some companies also have (or assign to the ESOP committee) the additional function of acting as a steering committee for employee involvement. These committees typically are responsible for structuring, evaluating, and changing the employee participation system. In some cases, they may also have some decision-making authority to implement ideas that come up from that process. Finally, they may interact with management to provide input and discuss strategic issues. Steering committees can add credibility to the employment involvement process and get input from a more representative group of people than just having management run the system.

Carris Reels in Rutland, Vermont, may have the most active employee steering committee. It started its ESOP in 1995 and became 100% ESOP-owned in 2008. The 500-employee company manufactures reels and other packaging products for the wire and cable industry, with its main operation in Rutland as well as eight divisions worldwide.

Table 9-1. Participation checklist

Work issue	Decides alone	Formally recommends to management	Has input only	Who is on team?
Human Resources				
Hiring, firing, or career development				
Selection or review of supervisors/management				
Work rules, vacation, benefits, compensation				
Complaint resolution procedures				
Worker training and evaluation				
Overseeing participation process				
Working Conditions and Work Design				
Product and service development				
Process change				
Process evaluation				
Customer service response				
Process and/or quality control				
Work space layout and design				
Supplier Relations				
Just-in-time or lean management				
Supplier quality assessment and improvement				
Selection of equipment				
Material tracking and use				
Customer Relations				
New customer development				
Customer service response and measurement				
Billing, collection, and contracts				
Corporate Issues				
Strategic issues				
Product/service development				
Corporate finance training				
Developing and using critical numbers				
Mission/value statements				
Information flows other than finance				
Marketing				
Safety				
Social events				
Healthcare/wellness programs				

When the ESOP was started, Bill Carris, the owner and CEO, set up a Long-Term Plan Committee to help design the ESOP and implement Carris' vision for the future of the company. Management initially appointed members to the committee from a broad cross-section of employees. Eventually, the committee merged with the Management Group, a committee of all division and site managers, to form the Corporate Steering Committee. In 1996, the committee members began to be elected by constituents.

About one-third of the committee is elected by employees from among their peers. The remaining members include corporate and site managers. Their charge is a wide one. They can help set overall corporate policies, and early on implemented such programs as the "inner circle" that allows employees to spend a week at another division and the "full circle" that sends people abroad to developing countries on paid time to learn about life and issues in these places. Employees report back on what they learned.

Most of the focus, however, is on education, training, employee involvement programs, and corporate policy. The group meets for two days twice a year. It can also create ad hoc subgroups to work on specific issues. The groups have appointed members from the committee, but anyone else can volunteer to join them.

Fixing Participation Problems

Sometimes companies embark on employee involvement programs only to run into a stone wall from managers, supervisors, and/or employees. "We tried that before," they say, "and it just didn't work." A lot of this frustration has to do with the inevitable ambiguity that arises when people's roles change. Managers and supervisors now are supposed to coach and listen; employees to share ideas and information.

Defining these new roles can be difficult, but it is essential to developing realistic expectations of just what participation involves. Typically, there's a learning curve for each of the groups. Management needs to learn how to balance giving up control while continuing to provide leadership. Middle managers must learn to give up some authority and become catalysts for employee input and decision making. Employees need to learn new skills that will allow them to contribute. Lastly, each group needs to understand how everyone else contributes.

Incentive Pay

A professor of organizational psychology was annoyed by students playing touch football every day outside his window and making a lot of noise. Rather than ask them to stop, he told them he loved what they were doing and would give them each $2 every day they played. They were very pleased, of course. The next week, he said he loved seeing them play, but could only afford $1. They grumbled a bit but kept on playing. The week after that, he told them he loved seeing them play but couldn't afford to pay them anymore. Disgruntled, they quit.

That may be an apocryphal story, but it illustrates a point made by Alfie Kohn, a leading scholar on incentive pay, and Daniel Pink, the best-selling author of *Drive*. They argue that incentive pay can turn the most powerful kind of motivation, which is intrinsic, into an externally driven and fragile incentive. Pink says that real motivation comes from autonomy, purpose, and challenge, all things the employee engagement ideas here help create (Pink is a fan of employee ownership).

Then there is the story of the Australian economist who wanted his toddler to keep his diaper dry, so he told him he could have a treat if he did that overnight. The toddler, who was no fool, took off his diaper. At work, incentive pay can have a similar effect—it gets people to pay more attention to one goal when they should be focusing on overall performance.

There are many strong proponents of incentive pay, however. One argument is not focused on motivation, but controlling costs. By structuring more pay as variable, companies have less risk that an off-year will force costly layoffs, while the bounty of good years is shared. Profit sharing is the logical way to do that. Think of it not so much as an incentive for behavior as a reward for prior efforts.

Incentives based on more specific measures (increasing sales, decreasing overhead, improving on-time delivery, etc.) are trickier. SRC Holdings has elegantly solved this problem by identifying one or two critical weaknesses each year and building an incentive around that. Part of the annual bonus comes from solving the weakness; part comes from profit sharing. Once the weakness has been solved, usually by some system change, a new one can be identified. Other companies, such as Pool Covers, use short-term games to address specific issues, but the rewards are more fun (such as shopping sprees or baseball tickets) than financially substantial.

There is no hard and fast rule on what will work for any company, but there are some key issues in any incentive system:

- Make sure people understand what the goal is, how it is measured, and why it matters.
- Post progress toward the goal regularly.
- Don't just ask people to work harder to achieve the goal. Find ways that people can share ideas about how to get there and give them tools to implement these ideas.

Conclusion

Creating high-engagement cultures is hard work. But it is work that pays off. At the NCEO, we know of very few companies that backed away from these systems once they started them, although they are often changed. It's common to start with one system, as at Phelps County Bank, then find as people get used to that, their skills and confidence rise to a level where a different system is needed.

High-engagement systems have been repeatedly shown to be the most effective intervention a company can create to improve performance. But go to an NCEO conference and witness the enthusiasm and energy coming from managers and employees of these companies and you'll learn something else—they are also the most fun way to run a company.

Case Studies

The two case studies below look at two of the many ways ESOP companies have moved to high-engagement systems.

Radian Research

In December 2008, Radian Research became 100% employee-owned when it purchased the shares of its founder, Glenn Mayfield. Radian is the leading manufacturer of testing equipment that assesses watt-hour calculation systems for utilities. The company now has approximately 100 employees at two locations in Lafayette, Indiana, and Jackson, Mississippi.

When Radian became an ESOP company, it started to move away from its traditional top-down management style. Soon after becoming employee-owned, an ESOP ambassador team was established to give all employees a clear communication channel. The team is composed of volunteer employee representatives like business development manager Renee Mundell and production supervisor Mark Billings. Representatives come from each department and from both nonmanagement and management positions.

Team members are responsible for far more than basic communications and education concerning the ESOP, however. They meet once a month to go over key metrics and track the progress of all new company goals and initiatives.

In 2014, Radian's Lafayette location began dividing employees into eight cross-functional groups with an employee from each department. One ESOP ambassador team member is leader for each group. The groups are responsible for tasks such as contributing a section to the company newsletter as well as meeting regular process improvement measures. These cross-functional groups carry out process walkthroughs in each department and provide suggestions on how these processes might be improved. This led to a complete restructuring of the company's assembly floor. Management may have helped facilitate this discussion, but employees were responsible for redesigning the layout and driving improvement.

Mundell and Billings tell a story about a time this culture of bottom-up engagement was put to the test. Radian employee-owner Rhonda Pope received a massive purchase order and realized that she and her team could not sufficiently wind so many transformers by their deadline. Instead of going to management to address the problem, Rhonda shut down her line, gathered her team, and asked management for some prints and materials. Management did not fully know what she was doing, but they provided her with the materials and let her take the lead. She sat down with her team to assess their process for winding transformers and looked for ways to improve it. They redesigned the process and met their deadline. The team's innovations were completely employee-driven and required only the trust and support of management to accomplish their goals effectively.

Steve Silver

Steve Silver Company (SSC), a wholesale furniture distributor specializing in casual dining, occasional, and home office furniture, became majority employee-owned in 2011 through an ESOP. Despite the turmoil in the housing and furniture markets in recent years, SSC and its 227 employees have experienced tremendous growth since becoming employee-owned with the help of education programs and engagement processes that have empowered employees to implement their innovative ideas.

David Corbin, COO at SSC, says that before becoming employee-owned in 2011, the company's mission was to turn a successful business into an even better and more consistently high-performing organization with a focus on innovation. SSC accomplished this by concentrating on two complementary process cycles. The first gave employees a stake in the business and its financial performance through employee ownership while training employees to think like business owners. The second taught employees to act like business owners through a process for implementing their ideas to improve company performance.

SSC's ESOP committee, which is made up of senior managers, midlevel managers, and warehouse workers, has several duties, one of which is designing and implementing the company's training program. The company's senior leadership team carries out the training program in two stages: initial onboarding training and ongoing training. The onboarding training starts with an owner's manual for all employee-owners, which is designed like a car owner's manual. The manual describes the mission and vision of the company, how the ESOP works, and the key players, and it also includes SSC's summary plan description. Ongoing training includes business update presentations, the SSC's ESOP communication website, and annual ESOP stock presentations with David Corbin and the company's independent trustee.

After the training sessions, employees are divided into innovation teams led by ESOP committee members. The teams carry out brainstorming sessions in which employees develop ideas and decide which new products, process improvements, or cost-saving ideas are most promising. The innovation teams then present these ideas to the ESOP committee, which passes them along to the senior leadership team for evaluation. At the start of the year, the senior leadership team considers all of the new innovative ideas that have been developed in both the onboarding and ongoing training programs and selects five or six major strategic innovation projects, or SIPs. Once the company's board approves these SIPs, they are implemented concurrently. The SIPs are implemented by cross-functional teams, which are composed of employee-owners who have a familiarity with the aspects of the business most affected by each new project.

Employees are empowered through a process known as the PDCA cycle, which stands for Plan, Do, Check and Learn, and Act. In this process cycle, the strategic innovation teams clearly state the problem (Plan), implement the improvement ideas (Do), assess what works and what does not work (Check and Learn), and either make the new method a measurable standard or repeat the process cycle (Act). In some cases, when implementing a new idea using the PDCA cycle, a new problem is revealed. When SSC started implementing a software system for real-time quality control reporting, the company found problems with some of their quality control processes during the Check and Learn step. Once the project had successfully been implemented, they were able to address additional problems that had been revealed during the process cycle. In the first two to three years after becoming employee-owned and implementing the PDCA cycles, SSC's value more than doubled.

KEY TAKEAWAYS

- ESOPs will contribute to better performance only if teamed with an active culture of employee engagement.
- Getting lots of small ideas from lots of people is your company's critical competitive advantage.
- Share at least basic data from your financial statements and teach people how to understand it.

- Create critical numbers at all levels to measure performance for workgroups and business functions.
- Participation does not happen just because you allow it. Open-door policies rarely mean much.
- To get employees engaged in sharing ideas and information, you must structure participation as part of the job. Focus on teams—ad hoc, workgroup, cross-functional, and whatever else works for you.
- Participation works better if employees are involved in structuring how the involvement systems work.
- Create checklists for where people do participate now and where they might in the future.
- Periodically assess how you are doing and what can be changed.

Chapter 10

Strategy and ESOP Sustainability

Ken Ritterspach[1]

In an ongoing study on employee engagement, Gallup has consistently reported a disturbing statistic that has only marginally gotten better since the beginning of the study in 2000. Fewer than 32% of American employees are "actively engaged" in their jobs as defined by their answers to a series of questions. Over 50% responded in a way that put them in the "not engaged" category. Perhaps the most startling statistic is that over 17% gave responses that pegged them as "actively disengaged." That means the actions of those employees are actually working against the betterment of the company, clearly not in the best interest of anyone!

ESOP companies have a tremendous potential advantage to create an alignment between management and ownership that can dramatically raise the level of engagement on strategy and planning at both the corporate and work group levels. It's not automatic, and it takes a concerted effort. In this chapter, we share the stories of three companies that have made the effort. The result is employees who are engaged because they have a vested interest in the long-term success of the company (i.e., the ultimate job security), and clearly see how they can contribute.

---

1. I wish to give a special thanks to Cecil Ursprung, the former CEO of Reflexite Corporation. Cecil provided the initial idea for this chapter and very valuable input in its development. He recently retired as CEO of Reflexite after 25 years. Reflexite's ESOP was established in 1984. Reflexite not only made the ESOP its largest shareholder, but also established other equity vehicles, including a stock option plan, an ESPP, and an internal market for the stock. Cecil is on the NCEO's board of directors and is active in the New England chapter of the ESOP Association. Cecil also serves on the boards of two ESOP companies.

The long-term engagement of employees directly impacts the sustainability of an ESOP. That engagement is determined by a multitude of factors: HR policies and practices, the alignment of decisions with company values, leaders "walking the talk," and the degree to which employees are empowered, to name a few. High on that list are strategic planning and implementation. Those functions touch many aspects of organizations, and they are foundational components of company results. The more effective the strategy function, the greater the likelihood of employee engagement and long-term sustainability.

Although the direct responsibility and final approval for strategy ultimately lies with the CEO and other members of the leadership and governance teams, the more that employees are involved, the greater the likelihood of buy-in, creativity, and enthusiastic engagement. Not surprisingly, these are key elements that drive sustainability.

Strategy: An Overview

Strategy is a favorite topic in the world of business. Each year, Fortune 500 companies spend millions of dollars and enlist hundreds of consultants to help with strategic planning. It is a staple of every business school curriculum and the subject of countless business management books. The tools of strategy are well established (and, unfortunately, simply their use is often confused with "being" strategic): SWOT Analysis, Five Forces, PEST Analysis, Balanced Scorecard, etc.

The strategic planning process can range from a week-long retreat of senior leaders at a Caribbean resort to an entrepreneur sitting at his or her laptop creating a one-page strategic plan with an online template.

At its most basic level, strategy refers to a set of activities that connects the current state of an organization to a desired future state. Those activities will vary depending on the industry, size of the company, stage of growth, etc. Strategy is how a company fulfills its mission in the largest context. If the mission is the "what we do" and the values are the "who we are," then strategy is the "how we do it."

Michael Robert described strategy as "Dealing with the environment for a while." "A while" because strategy is not static. Technology evolves, competitors come and go, customers change, markets evolve—nothing is static. Accordingly, how companies interact with the business environment needs to constantly be examined and adjusted to achieve both the short-term and long-term goals of the organization.

Strategy is big picture, not narrowly focused. Forecasting, setting objectives, budgeting, and operational excellence are all important ingredients. But they are incomplete from a strategic point of view. Also, they tend to be quantitative. The heart of strategy is qualitative.

The strategy function depends on many factors. Typically, the larger the company, the more complex the strategy function, the more quantitative, the more formal. Often, the driving strategy for smaller companies is simply making payroll! As companies get larger and more complex, the strategy function evolves. The same is true for ESOP companies—each one is different. However, in general, ESOP companies are smaller: more than 90% of ESOP companies have less than $200 million in revenue. That affords them the advantage of making the strategy function more accessible to a larger number of employees

This chapter does not summarize the classical treatment of strategy in the business literature (Cotter, Hamel, Porter, Robert, etc.). Instead, the purpose here is to focus on the unique attributes and requirements that are either particularly relevant to ESOPs or unique to them (e.g., the repurchase obligation).

Strategy and ESOPs: A New Frontier

The difference in strategy between ESOP and non-ESOP companies is primarily one of degree. The key principles of effective strategy processes and tools apply to any company regardless of ownership. However, an ESOP has a unique opportunity (and responsibility) to invigorate the strategy function by harnessing the brainpower, energy, and commitment of employee-owners. Engaging employees in the strategy process at the appropriate level is a hallmark of enlightened leadership. It is smart business. In ESOP companies, engaging employees in the strategy process has even more potential since employee-owners can more readily see their own financial best interests as part of the strategy discussion. By virtue of their size, smaller ESOP companies can more easily engage employees in the strategy process. Communication is more direct and easily carried out, there is less bureaucracy, employees can more readily share what they know about the business, and there is less "emotional distance" between senior management and other levels of the organization. For many ESOP companies, there is a new, untapped frontier in participation: involvement by virtually all employees in various phases of strategic planning and implementation, especially the latter. By its very definition, strategic implementation is important work, and there is a never-ending source of content. The strategy function, properly understood and managed, is self-perpetuating. Planning each year generates new priorities for implementation at all levels of the company: corporate, departments, teams, cells, etc. Employees can easily be involved in all phases of implementation.

Employee engagement can begin early in the transition process. In fact, the roots of sustainability are in the strategic planning that occurs before establishing the ESOP. Many experts agree that the most difficult maneuver any business makes is the transition from the founder to the next generation of management. The founder must be willing to hand over power to new leaders for the management of his or her "child," which may have taken 30 years of effort to nurture to maturity. At the same time, the business is likely losing its chief strategist and a considerable source of financing. What better way to manage the transition than a broad-based effort to develop and implement a strategy that the new owners help develop?

Consider the success story of Carris Reels, an employee-owned company whose ESOP evolution began as the brainchild of founder Bill Carris. A colleague recalled, "Bill had lots of brilliant ideas, so I didn't pay much attention to the ESOP idea when he first raised it. Actually, by that time, he had been working for several years, talking with business people, academics, family and friends." Careful thought and research paved the way for future success.

The first formal phase was a two-year period of Bill working with the management team on a Long-Term Plan document that was the blueprint for the evolution of the ESOP. During that time, management got up to speed, attending ESOP conferences and meeting people from other employee-owned companies.

More importantly, Bill began meeting with groups of employees from around the company. One of his priorities was to have a very inclusive process. It wasn't to be "Bill's ESOP." Rather, employee-owners were to make the important decisions. The planning committee was large and broad-based, representing all sites and all three shifts. Bill mandated only two provisions: there was to be one vote for each employee-owner, and the company would donate a percentage of annual profits to charity. The rest was up to the planning committee.

The Long-Term Plan called for transactions over a period of many years—from 1995 to 2008, when it became 100% employee-owned. It also outlined a mission, values and guiding principles, a vision, and operating processes. Most importantly, it set the expectation that employees would be heavily involved in both strategic planning and implementation. For example:

- Shortly after the ESOP was formed, the ESOP committee and the site management teams were merged, thereby creating a Corporate Steering Committee. The CSC has some direct decision making powers, but its highest use is as an advisory committee to senior management and the board of directors.

- Each of the company's eight sites has its own strategic planning committee, of which one member is the CSC representative. Most of what occurs at the site planning committees is operational in nature, which includes setting annual goals, preparing budgets, and monitoring progress. Each site holds a monthly employee-owner meeting.

- Each of the eight sites conducts its site planning differently, depending on its needs. Although some sites are more inclusive and transparent than others, there is a wide range of input from employee-owners into the strategic planning and review process.

- Non-executive management and executive managers serve together on the ESOP trustee committee.

- In 2014 non-executive management and executive managers began serving together as part of a new seven-member board of directors.

A total commitment to the principles of employee ownership by Bill Carris paved the way to innovative and creative ways to ensure that employee-owners are actively involved in both strategic planning and implementation.

Planning

Strategic planning includes five fundamental phases that are generally applicable across all industries.

Market analysis. The strategy of a company is always a function of the market in which it operates. Companies exist to fill an unmet need, sometimes known, sometimes unknown. In his classic strategy analysis, Michael Porter identified five market forces: the threat of established rivals, the threat of substitute products, the threat of new entrants, the bargaining power of suppliers, and the bargaining power of customers.

In an ESOP, typically the original market analysis took place when the founder(s) started the company. On a continuing basis, the purpose of the market analysis is to continually monitor the business environment.

Assessment. Building on the analysis of the market is an overall assessment of both internal and external factors that affect the future success of the organization. The classic tool in assessment is a SWOT (Strengths, Weaknesses, Opportunities, and Threats) analysis.

- *Strengths:* internal capabilities and assets that provide a competitive advantage.
- *Weaknesses:* functions or characteristics of a company that make it vulnerable in the marketplace.
- *Opportunities:* aspects of the external market that an organization can exploit to its benefit.
- *Threats:* external elements (companies, products, technologies, etc.) to which the company is vulnerable.

For an ESOP company, conducting the SWOT analysis has the potential to be a much more robust process, simply by having employee-owners actively engaged at all levels. Employees know firsthand the strengths and weaknesses of the company. There are specific departments and teams (notably sales personnel) that have industry knowledge that probably equals the intelligence from many trade specialists. And the information is free for the asking! The process to elicit the information from employees can be to simply ask them: brainstorming sessions, internal focus groups, etc.

Marketing strategy. Defining the target customer (who are they, where are they, why do they buy from you, etc.), articulating the attributes that make your company unique, creating your "brand" in the marketplace, etc.

Medium-term picture. Typically this is a three- to five-year vision of how big the company will be (employees, locations, product lines, etc.), revenue size, and key attributes. Strategically, it creates a more granular picture for employees than the long-term target. It also serves to inform the one-year plan. For ESOP companies, the medium-term picture includes the repurchase obligation.

Vision. What is the company going to look like in the future, both long term and short term? There are three key components in setting the vision:

- *Values:* These define your culture. The values are "who" you are as a company. Identifying values is a discovery process. It's not the work of a committee or the CEO who "declares" the values. Here's a simple exercise to uncover those values. Identify a star employee—someone whom everybody would identify as a major contributor in the organization, regardless of position or function, a "go-to" person. What are the four or five attributes of that individual? How would you describe him/her to a third party? Those descriptors are generally the core values of the organization.

- *Focus:* Gino Wickman, author of the book *Traction*, breaks this into two components: your cause/passion/purpose (the "why" of the organization) and your niche: what do you do to carry out that purpose. The power of focus is twofold: it keeps the collective attention of the company pointing in the same direction, and it also serves as a filter for initiatives that can distract an organization and take it off target in achieving its mission.

- Long-term target: The longer-term horizon is different for each company. For some it might be 10 years, for others 5, and for yet others 15. The concept behind a long-term target is to give employees a bigger, more exciting picture of a future state, to feel as though they are part of something greater than having a job with a paycheck.

Obviously for ESOP companies, the incentive to be part of the conversation around the long-term target is greater because of the ownership factor. ESOP companies can play off that incentive by including employees in the process of painting the target. Specific roles can include conducting market research, helping with scenario planning, developing forecasting models, generating options for products and services, creating "what-if" models, etc.

When the vision of a company comes to life in the hearts and minds of employee-owners, the results can be dramatic. Recology is a San Francisco solid-waste processing firm that conducts collection, sorting, transfer, and landfill management. In June 2013 it was facing an expiration date for its contract to collect trash for Vacaville, California. The municipal government had earlier decided to open up the contract to new bidders. Three new bids came in to the city council, and the municipal staff recommended one of them over Recology. It wasn't that Recology was disliked; it was just cold, hard dollars and cents. The recommended vendor would net the city $1.1 million in savings compared to the status quo.

At the city council meeting to award the contract, an army of citizens and employees spoke up in support of continuing the city's contract with Recology. They ranged from customers, who had grown to appreciate the quality service they received, to Recology employees, who were well known in the community. The local newspaper characterized the display as "an outcry of public support." The council heard "emotional pleas by employees, residents and folks from other cities speaking on behalf of Recology. Speakers pointed to the sense of community the company had with Vacaville after more than 50 years of service."

Ultimately, this show of support for Recology carried the day. The council voted unanimously to stick with Recology. It was a victory for the citizens who turned out to speak, but beyond that, it was a validation of Recology's long-standing investment of time and effort to develop a relationship with its community and its customers.

Also, Recology's success was largely driven by a pride of ownership that comes from being an employee-owned company. Julia Lopez, a Recology employee, summed it up best when she spoke at the city council meeting. She looked at the city council members and the competitors in the room and stated: "You can hire some of our employees back, but you won't have the same level of service. That kind of service only comes when you have the entire team. We think of ourselves as a family. If staff's recommendation goes through, you will break up the family and you lose the team."

For Recology, its strong enthusiasm for being 100% employee-owned translated into a positive relationship with neighbors, customers, and municipalities. This personal touch is hard to find, and it's valuable. For the city of Vacaville, it was worth more than $1.1 million. For Recology, it meant a renewed 10-year contract.

Employee-owned companies that get to know and respect their customers have an advantage that competitors can't match.

Implementation

Strategic implementation converts strategy from planning to realization. A plan without execution is wishful thinking. The key elements of strategic implementation include the issues below.

One-Year Plan with Budgets

This is the transitional document between planning and implementation. The plan includes revenue numbers, profitability targets, and objectives for the year. Ideally, the objectives are SMART: Specific, Measurable, Attainable, Relevant, and Time-Driven. The budget is a statement of both the sources and uses of funds that are required to meet the objectives.

Strategic Initiatives

Companies undertake specific projects, above and beyond producing goods and services in the normal course of business. Some initiatives are planned at the beginning of the year. Others are created to respond to the inevitable changes in the business climate. Initiatives are the heart of strategic implementation. Unless resources (including time) are allocated, initiatives rarely succeed.

In ESOP companies, employee-owners not only carry out these initiatives as members of project teams; they are also an excellent source of creating them in the first place by identifying specific needs, defining requirements, specifying resources, eliciting approvals from senior management, gaining buy-in from other employees, etc.

Wickman advocates the creation of "Rocks," 90-day projects carefully chosen as the most important (i.e., most strategic) initiatives for the company.

Scorecard

A scorecard is a set of activity-based numbers that predict future outcomes. Scorecard numbers are different than financial reporting. For example, sales for the month is an example of a number that is typically part of financial reporting. In order to predict what the sales number will be (and therefore have an opportunity to affect it), companies might track the number of cold calls, leads generated, hits on the website, proposals submitted, etc. These are examples of scorecard numbers.

For an ESOP, the scorecard is an excellent tool to strengthen the relationship between managers and other employee-owners. A scorecard number for the company is a function of what individual departments, teams, and even individuals do. Employees feel empowered when they see the link between what they're doing and the overall results of the company.

Issue Resolution

Inevitably, there are obstacles to a company's achieving its desired results. Production problems, loss of a customer, market changes, employees leaving—the list can be overwhelming. The effectiveness and efficiency of how issues get resolved plays a big role in the success and long-term health of an organization. Employee-owners have a vested interest in helping issues get resolved. Lower-level employees often see problems more quickly than managers; they also have a good grasp of root causes and effective solutions.

Market Intelligence

A key driver in a change to a company's strategy is activity in the marketplace. Changes in the competitive landscape, the arrival or departure of major customers, evolutions in technology, and changes overseas are just some examples of marketplace disruptions that can affect company strategy.

Maintaining a disciplined process to monitor outside influences can often spell the difference between success and failure. ESOP committees by their nature tend to have an inward focus. The most successful ones, however, share the responsibility of management of being constantly aware of what is happening *externally* that might affect the long-term and short-term health of the organization.

Change Management

Extensive work has been done on the subject of change management. Any successful strategic implementation process includes a successful change management policy. Defining the change, planning for it, and implementing the change can be simple or complicated depending on many factors. Regardless of complexity, the entire process is enhanced with active involvement by employees at all levels of the company. Again, ESOP companies have an added advantage. Employee-owners who have been involved in strategic planning, initiatives, staying in tune with the marketplace, etc., are going to understand the need for change and the importance of its effective implementation.

Forecasting

Forecasting tools range from simple to complex, depending on the needs of the organization and nature of the marketplace. The fundamental components are accurate and timely "period to date" financials (i.e., financial and other results for a given time period). Based on an accurate history and market intelligence about future company results, a forecast produces a picture of anticipated results. Predictions of future results are rarely a simple reflection of past history, although such "straight-line" calculations can give a starting point. Seasonality, the current status of major customers (good or bad), and new product introductions by significant competitors are examples of outside factors that can affect future results. The key to successful forecasting is having a process in which data is systematically collected *and* analyzed.

Risk Management

Risk management can be broadly defined as any activity with balance sheet implications, ranging from the purchase of insurance to the investment in redundancy assets. This is an area in which significant differences can exist between ESOP and non-ESOP companies, simply because ownership is spread over larger numbers. In a company with one or several owners, the tolerance for risk can be calculated relatively easily, and the level of tolerance is generally higher. With large numbers of owners and therefore a wide range of interests and needs, it is more difficult to ascertain the appetite for risk. As a result, leadership teams, boards, and trustees need to exert special caution with activities that have more risk. Specifically, the ownership of an ESOP rests in a retirement plan trust for the employee-owners. There is a fiduciary responsibility to manage risk prudently.

Repurchase Obligation

Chapter three of this book looks at this issue in detail. Clearly, however, because the repurchase obligation affects cash flow and reserves, it needs to be carefully factored into any strategic decisions. This is largely not an issue for non-ESOP companies. ESOP companies face repurchase obligations in drips and drabs over time; non-ESOP private companies face them all at once and often build their strategies around a goal of an ultimate sale. These varying time frames create potentially very divergent paths.

Strategy in Action

A great example of a comprehensive strategy is Web Industries, a 500-employee, flexible material converting and end-product contract manufacturer based in Massachusetts, with plants in several states.

Web Industries believes that successful strategic implementation is ultimately in the hands of employees. When employees understand, are committed to, and (most importantly), can adjust and adapt a strategy to the particulars of real-world circumstances, then strategy has a high probability of success. Accordingly, Web has evolved a highly participative strategy deployment process to engage all employees in strategy implementation. Their process has several key features:

- *Selecting plans.* Every October on ESOP Day, each site mixes its staff into small groups of 8 to 10. With trained facilitators, these groups prioritize and choose proposed "A3 focus areas" for the coming year. ("A3" refers to a collaborative, in-depth problem-solving process originally developed by Toyota.) The groups then report out their top three choices and the rationale for the choices. The insight and strategic alignment demonstrated by these teams always surprises the many visitors on hand for ESOP Day festivities.

- *Simple written A3 plans.* Web uses a simple one-page A3 plan format posted in every site. The plans include a story (why this strategy matters), key metrics, and a visual roadmap of key implementation milestones with SMART (Specific, Measurable, Attainable, Relevant, and Time-driven) goals and names of volunteer team members responsible for each element.

- *Monthly report-outs.* Every month, non-management "reporting owners" meet with the teams, assess and record progress on goals, and report out to both the site leadership team and to plant meetings on every shift. The reporting owners grow in their leadership skills by fielding questions from the staff and adopting a healthy outsider's perspective to challenge their teams.

- *Excellence and fun.* The character of the process can feel like MBA-seminar-meets-comedy-club. There is a seriousness of purpose as employee-owners engage deeply in matters of tremendous importance to them, and a playful, joyful good cheer as they support, encourage, and banter with their colleagues.

The A3 strategy deployment process is one of many structured approaches Web uses to embed employee engagement into its culture. The A3's provide a safe forum for everyone to ask questions, to get answers from people they know and trust, and to express opinions that get taken seriously. All of this helps overcome resistance to change, which can otherwise be a huge drag on strategy. On a practical level, the A3's drive completion of goals, accountability, and results.

Web's experience with highly engaged employee-owners using A3's for strategy deployment has coincided with significant strategic advantages in its key markets.

Hallmarks of Great Strategy in ESOPs

There is no better environment than an ESOP company for strategic planning and implementation to thrive. It begins with an alignment between management and ownership, which infuses a natural energy into the strategic planning process. Employees have an incentive to provide input as well as critical thinking. That energy continues into the implementation of strategy, where again, employee-owners have a vested interest in being sure that plans are executed. When plans are executed well, results improve, job satisfaction increases, engagement becomes energized, and concerns about job security decrease.

Due to broad ownership and variable sophistication among participants, the attributes of strategic planning and implementation are especially important in an ESOP. Here are some hallmarks of great strategy in ESOPs:

- *Keep it simple.* Organizations and leaders tend toward complexity. It's hard enough to create momentum, much less when plans are not intuitively understood. Less is more.

- *Communicate often and well.* Communication opens the floodgates to engagement and maximizing the human capital provided by an ESOP. Involvement in the strategic planning process provides a direct line of sight to company success, which in turn promotes security and sustainability. That puts special pressure on effective communication, both in frequency and mode. Unless you "over communicate," you can't engage employee-owners, thereby negating the strategic advantages available to an ESOP. Research says that someone needs to hear a message seven times before it's really heard.

- *Think qualitative, not quantitative.* It's relatively easy to play with forecasts, models, sensitivity analysis, and all the other powerful tools associated with strategic planning. However, the meat of strategy is qualitative, answering the hard questions about things like targeted customers, product modification, honest competitive analysis, and core competencies. Tools are simply that. If the underlying processes for planning are not in place, it doesn't matter how elegant or sophisticated the tools are.

- *Be data-driven.* While communicating about how the company is doing requires qualitative thinking, corporate strategy needs to focus on numbers as well. Metrics strip away all the subjectivity and politics about what's working and what's not. The numbers don't lie. Being strategic is a disciplined, rational process. Collecting reliable data over time in a consistent manner gives the basis for making informed decisions.
- *Change carefully.* Strategy should change only when the marketplace changes and/or there are significant changes internally (e.g., size and maturity of the company).
- *Use divergent and convergent thinking, in that order.* The early stages of successful planning are often aided by divergent thinking: looking outside the box, not being limited by simply what has worked in the past. The final stages of planning and then implementation, however, require convergent thinking and discipline. Successful companies have a relentless obsession to simplify and to focus. You can't do it all. Pick what you're passionate about and what you do better than anyone else. Then do a lot of it.

A Final Word

The sustainability of an ESOP company ultimately hinges on the employee-owners' level of commitment. Commitment doesn't happen overnight, but it's well worth the wait and the effort. Sometimes it produces truly heroic efforts.

On a hot Sunday afternoon, a 343-acre fire blazed through an area around Auburn, California, destroying 63 homes and threatening the property of Recology. Charlie Onthank, a shift supervisor, was working nearby and saw flames along a perimeter fence, threatening the entire fleet of Recology trucks. Some were already on fire. Onthank knew he had to save as many trucks as he could by moving them away from the fence's flames and getting the burning ones away from the petroleum tanks resting near the facility. If he didn't act fast, the whole facility and its fleet could explode.

"I got into the Cat and pushed the burning truck and the burning toters into a pile and dug a fire line around the transfer trail." Two-year employee Cesar Delgado, who runs the facility's entrance booth, joined the effort. Without hesitation, he worked alongside Onthank to move the trucks, sometimes driving them while they were on fire, away from the approaching flames. "I knew I had to save the trucks and the business, because the company is our life," said Delgado. He recalled seeing flames 50 feet in the air and watching them through his rear-view mirror while he drove. "But I just kept moving," he said.

Though not scheduled for a shift that day, Carlos Robles, who lives nearby, saw the smoke and left immediately. Robles somehow got through the road blockade and helped the others by hosing down the trucks. When he arrived, three trucks had burned, but all he had on his mind was saving what he could. "This is our life," Robles said. "I came to the lunch room to breathe and wrapped a shirt around my face. All the while, we had our personal vehicles parked and running as an exit option in case it got too bad."

Fortunately, it never reached that point. These employee-owners were able to save the fleet and the facility from the fire's destruction without any injuries. General Manager John Rowe arrived on the scene after coming from Sacramento, parking his car and running to get to the facility. "Things were in really good shape. These guys care about each other."

Onthank, whom the others call the leader, is humble about his role as hero: "We did what we needed, so the shop wouldn't burn." Today 85 employees are thankful for their fellow employee-owners' success in saving the trucks and facility from the fire. Their efforts maintained their jobs and a company that they are proud to proclaim as employee-owned.

KEY TAKEAWAYS

- *ESOP companies face all the same strategic concerns as non-ESOP companies.* Because of repurchase obligation issues, ESOPs have to think differently about the use of cash.

- *Employee ownership offers an important opportunity to generate more employee involvement at all levels in the strategic process, creating more ideas and better feedback.*

- *Unlike non-ESOP companies that usually communicate minimally about strategy, ESOP companies need to take this opportunity to make employees feel like owners.*

SUGGESTED READING

Lencioni, Patrick. *The Five Dysfunctions of a Team.* Jossey-Bass, 2002.

Porter, Michael E. "What Is Strategy?" *Harvard Business Review,* Nov.-Dec. 1996.

Robert, Michel. *Strategic Thinking.* DPI, 1985

Wickman, Gino. *Traction: Get a Grip on Your Business.* BenBella Books, 2011.

ACKNOWLEDGEMENTS

Thanks to the contributors of our company stories:

Web Industries: Michael Quarrey and Donnie Romine
Carris Reels: Dave Fitzgerald
Recology: Mark Romele

Ken Ritterspach is an executive consultant at Platinum Group. For more than 30 years, Ken Ritterspach has been leading middle-market companies as a CEO/president, as a business advisor, and as the owner of his own business. He has been the CEO of a 100% ESOP-owned company and worked in manufacturing, distribution, service, and public sector organizations. He works side-by-side with leaders and teams to analyze complex situations, develop and execute strategic plans, and gain buy-in for change. He has a strong history of speaking and facilitation, including seven years as a presenter and account manager for Franklin Covey. As a Certified Implementer for EOS Worldwide, Ken is passionate about helping leaders and teams maximize operating results. Ken received his BA from Yale and MBA (finance) and PhD (education) from Stanford.

Appendix

Additional Resources

NCEO Publications and Surveys

All of the NCEO resources below can be bought at nceo.org.

Governance and Fiduciary Issues

The ESOP Company Board Handbook looks at the corporate and ESOP responsibilities for board members, discusses how to think about executive pay, reports on interviews with a number of outside directors, provides templates for responding to acquisition offers, and more. The final chapter provides a detailed review of ESOP basics for board members.

The Inside ESOP Fiduciary Handbook is meant to provide an overview of life as an inside ESOP fiduciary. It alerts the reader to the key issues, including ESOP basics, fiduciary issues, valuation, and valuation scenarios that fiduciaries may face, along with board-trustee interactions and fiduciary insurance. Appendices provide sample DOL investigative questions, a sample trustee engagement letter, and a sample trust agreement.

ESOPs and Corporate Governance was written to help ESOP companies think through their governance issues. An important part of the book is a survey on governance practices in ESOP companies. It provides details on board compensation and composition, trustee selection and responsibilities, and employee roles on boards. Other chapters deal with how to select an ESOP trustee, legal obligations of the trustee under ERISA and as a shareholder, best practices for ESOP boards, and special legal considerations for the governance of ESOP companies.

Responding to Acquisition Offers in an ESOP Company reviews the legal requirements for boards and plan fiduciaries in vetting and negotiating offers. When a sale does occur, what administrative steps need to be taken? How should companies communicate with employees about their policies upon being acquired, as well as when an acquisition is in the works?

Our *ESOP Executive Compensation Survey* is done biannually and reports on how companies with ESOPs are compensating executives at seven key levels. It is customizable by region, industry, number of employees, revenue, pretax profits, S or C corporation status, and percentage owned by the ESOP.

Repurchase Obligations

How ESOP Companies Handle the Repurchase Obligation combines practical discussions with research in exploring the repurchase obligation and how it can be planned for and dealt with. A major feature of the fourth edition is a detailed report on the NCEO's most recent survey of how ESOP companies handle their repurchase obligations. The report is accompanied by dozens of pages of detailed tables.

Culture and Communications

The ESOP Committee Guide is the definitive guide to creating, developing, and maintaining a successful ESOP committee, with information on everything from determining the mission of the committee to ensuring its continued effectiveness in the face of difficulties.

The ESOP Communications Sourcebook provides a jump start to your ESOP communications by giving you (1) chapters about how to communicate employee ownership and financial issues; (2) templates of short documents (included in word-processing format on the CD as well as in the printed book) you can customize and use as handouts, intranet resources, or newsletter articles; and (3) sample communication documents from ESOP companies in digital form on the CD.

The Ownership Culture Survey is a fully customizable, comprehensive survey to give you the tools to most effectively measure your employee ownership culture. Survey results include comparison data from over 15,000 respondents at over 89 companies, with over 150 survey items to choose from. You receive an easy-to-understand report with specific recommendations based on your results and an hour of consultation.

Other Recommended Reading

Jack Stack and Bo Burlingham, *The Great Game of Business* (Crown Business, 2013): This classic book was updated for its 20th anniversary edition. It tells the story of how Springfield ReManufacturing Corporation, now SRC Holdings, used open-book management to grow from a 119-employee division of International Harvester about to close to a 100% ESOP company with over 1,200 employees. It provides very specific ideas on how to teach and use numbers at the workplace level.

Dean Schroeder and Alan Robinson, *Ideas Are Free* (Berrett-Koehler Publishers, 2004): This is essential reading for any company seeking to create ways for employees to have more input into how to make their company better. Unlike most management books, it provides a wide array of specific practices that have worked for companies of all sizes.

About the Author

Corey Rosen is the founder and former executive director of the National Center for Employee Ownership (NCEO) and now is its senior staff member. He cofounded the NCEO in 1981 after working for five years as a professional staff member in the US Senate, where he helped draft legislation on employee ownership plans. Before that, he taught political science at Ripon College. He is the author or coauthor of over 100 articles and many books on employee ownership, and a coauthor (with John Case and Martin Staubus) of *Equity: Why Employee Ownership Is Good for Business* (Harvard Business School Press, 2005). He has lectured on employee ownership on six continents, has appeared frequently on CNN, PBS, NPR, MSNBC, and other network programs, and is regularly quoted in the *Wall Street Journal,* the *New York Times, BusinessWeek,* and other leading publications. He holds a PhD in political science from Cornell University.

About the NCEO

The National Center for Employee Ownership (NCEO) is widely considered to be the leading authority on employee ownership in the U.S. and the world. Established in 1981 as a nonprofit information and membership organization, it now has over 2,500 members, including companies, professionals, unions, government officials, academics, and interested individuals. It is funded entirely through the work it does.

The NCEO's mission is to provide the most objective, reliable information possible about employee ownership at the most affordable price possible. As part of the NCEO's commitment to providing objective information, it does not lobby or provide ongoing consulting services. The NCEO publishes a variety of materials on employee ownership and participation; holds dozens of seminars, Webinars, and conferences on employee ownership annually; and offers online courses. The NCEO's work also includes extensive contacts with the media, both through articles written for trade and professional publications and through interviews with reporters.

Membership Benefits

NCEO members receive the following benefits:

- The members-only newsletter *Employee Ownership Report.*
- Access to the members-only area of the NCEO's Web site.
- Free access to live Webinars.
- Discounts on books and other NCEO products and services.
- The right to contact the NCEO for answers to questions.

An introductory one-year membership costs $90 for U.S. residents. To join or order publications, telephone us at 510-208-1300 or visit our Web site at www.nceo.org, which provides news updates and hundreds of articles as well as information on the many ways in which we can assist companies exploring employee ownership.